Beyond Federation:

Options to renew Australia's 1901 Constitution

Beyond Federation:

Options to renew Australia's 1901 Constitution

Editoral team: Klaas Woldring (managing editor)
Anthony Nicholas
Jim Snow
Mark Drummond

www.beyondfederation.org.au

www.beyondfederation.org.au

Cover Design by BookPOD

Printed and bound in Australia by BookPOD

A Catalogue-in-Publication is available from the National Library of Australia.

ISBN: 978-0-9941871-0-9

eISBN: 978-0-9941871-1-6

This book is dedicated to the memory of
Anthony Robert Nicholas (1929-2014),
an inspiration to us all.

Contents

Preface

Margaret Nicholas

In this electronic age since 2002, a small group of citizens from diverse locations have corresponded by email to share their ideas about improving governance in Australia under the label "Beyond Federation".

The group agrees that the Constitution of 1901 has passed its use-by-date and that state governments should be phased out. The essays in this eBook are the individual ideas of some of those correspondents plus a number of related statements by others. The aim of this eBook is to inform and stimulate its readers' interest in the governance of Australia, beyond federation.

Introduction

Rewriting the Australian Constitution

Geoff Armstrong

The current Australian Constitution was drafted during the 1890s by a small group of politicians, mainly representatives of the colonies that became the six states, who were committed to basing it on British parliamentary models and precedents dating back to well before the colony of New South Wales was established in 1788, and to retaining the rights already achieved by the states prior to talk of federation. With both anti-British sentiment and support for a republican Australia increasing in the mid-nineteenth century, one senior British politician said in the 1850s that he hoped to see '*democracy checked in the colony by stable institutions...*'. His goal was well on the way towards being realized when it was recommended in the final 1899 draft Australian Constitution that the states, each with its own Constitution, parliamentary structure, and approved rights, be retained in a federation structure. This proposal was put to a referendum with little community debate or input, and was adopted in 1901. The divisive creation of a federation made up of individual federal, state and territory governments contributed to impeding the progress of democracy in Australia, and the restrictive constraints that Section 128 of the Constitution applied to amendment of the 1901 Constitution made any subsequent beneficial improvement extremely difficult.

When the Constitution was being drafted in such a rapidly changing world, good planning should have anticipated and ensured that provision would be made for necessary amendments to be included. The 1901 Constitution was not well planned, and no such provision was made.

Prior to 1901 our nation had already been involved in wars, depressions and booms, and since federation it has experienced further dramatic changes to the world's as well as to Australia's environmental, social, political

1

and financial landscapes. Since adoption of the Constitution there has been commendable if slow social progress in Australia, with recognition of our Aboriginal population as fully entitled citizens, and growing acknowledgment of the constitutional rights of women and disabled and disadvantaged citizens. But throughout the same period there has been massive, continuing world environmental damage, largely resulting from out of control world population growth; refugee numbers have escalated worldwide as a result of deepening poverty in poorer countries, and the many wars between and within nations exercising their own interpretations of religious and political rights.

A Constitution for a Changed World

In the face of these changes, to now claim that the 1901 Constitution is still relevant in meeting Australia's needs in the twenty-first century is politically naïve and dangerously misleading, particularly when these attitudes adversely affect Australia's recognition and contribution as a responsible member of the international community. The current Australian Constitution has long been an outdated, dysfunctional nineteenth century British dominated model. The entire Constitution must be rewritten, not just by politicians, but also democratically by all Australians, and replaced as soon as may be. It is our need, our right, and our responsibility. It will no doubt be asked:

> *"But why rewrite the entire Constitution? Wouldn't it be simpler to just amend the faulty bits?"*

There are many reasons why this seemingly logical approach, which admittedly is the one supported by many constitutional academics, would not work. These reasons are too numerous and complex to explore in this simple introduction, but the structure, content, and restraints on change written into the 1901 Constitution make it certain that a clause-by-clause process would be sure to fail, or would be unacceptably delayed. On the other hand, rewriting and adopting a completely new Constitution containing a democratic amendment process would not preclude subsequent amendment to individual clauses if found necessary. That would be a win-win situation in contrast to the repeated clause-by-clause referendum failures that have been experienced during the last 114 years.

This book has been prepared to improve the knowledge of its readers about constitutional matters, and to encourage them as a matter of urgency to participate in producing a new Constitution which will ensure that our nation will become a fully sovereign twenty-first century democracy at last. Our new national Constitution must be democratically designed to lead Australia into the future. In doing this, it must also consider the views of those who are not yet entitled to vote, and anticipate the forecast needs of future citizens. It should set out the peoples' rights and responsibilities, display to all the philosophy on which management of our nation is based, spell out the principles by which members of our government must be guided, encourage them to discard adversarial politics and accept that it is their responsibility to unite our nation, not to divide it. Our national Constitution should be presented in a form readable by the people, so that they can relate to it, understand it, and support it. It must give them the right to initiate amendments, and to respond to any changes proposed by others.

The current Australian Constitution does none of these things. It was not written to present day democratic standards, and is now a historical anachronism that encourages us to live in the past. It never was adopted and 'owned' in its present form by the Australian people. In 2008, now High Court Justice Robert French said *"those who voted in 1899/1900 were defined by a limited franchise..."* while Justice Anthony Mason said that it received *"...no more than grudging acceptance by the people stemming from the absence of any other preferred model..."* The majority of Australians have shown little interest in the document since, and many reluctantly participate in elections and referendums only because it is compulsory. This must change in the twenty first century.

This book has been produced in 'voters' language to ensure that all citizens will get its message, understand the present and future content and importance of our Constitution, and become eager to participate in this review of its present omissions and flaws. To encourage and support this review, alternative models of government and alternative approaches to Australia's constitutional challenges generally are presented in relevant chapters as you read through.

However, it is stressed that the book has been written to guide, not to dictate the content of our new Constitution. That must remain the privilege of the people, and the responsibility of the parliament, both government and other elected representatives (let's discard the title of 'Opposition') to facilitate adherence to that principle. We must all, not only politicians and voters, but whole families, students, the media, educators, all of us – become involved this time, and contribute to make this **OUR AUSTRALIAN CONSTITUTION.**

Chapter 1

Replacing federation - aiming at decentralization

Klaas Woldring

In recent years a number of former politicians have condemned the continuation of federation for very good reasons. However, at the same time, others and some change-resistant scholars have argued that federalism still has something to offer and that the problems are either imagined and/or insignificant. Therefore, they claim, federalism can be 'modernized', 'repaired', 'saved', 'rescued' or 'made to work'. In a 2012 text edited by Kildea, Lynch and Williams [1], various arguments are put forward to show how 'practical' reforms may be achieved. The title *"Tomorrow's Federation"* suggests that Federation will continue but its major problems may be overcome by more pragmatic piecemeal tinkering. This looks much like capitulation; it suggests that many of the authors believe that major constitutional change is simply not possible. A quite different position is taken in this book. Not only is it regarded as possible but also as essential that it happens. There is a limit to 'pragmatism'. The cost of federation is staggering and the lack of effective decentralization in Australia is directly attributable to federation.

A spectacular number of federal-state money wasting and looming crises have emerged in federal Australia. They have rumbled on in major and minor public policy areas in recent decades, health services being the most spectacular, transport difficulties a close second. This situation, thankfully, has prompted considerable research about alternatives and public attitudes, amongst others by specialists at Griffith University. The PhD thesis by Mark Drummond (2007) provides convincing evidence that federal government

---

1   Paul Kildea, Andrew Lynch and George Williams (eds) (2012), Tomorrow's Federation, Federation Press.

has become extremely costly and is broken. Overall the results demonstrate that there is much dissatisfaction amongst the general public with federal-state relations as well. Also, a number of research papers have appeared of the conservative kind, such as the work by Anne Twomey and Glenn Withers (2007), which aims to show that some other federations are doing well and that there is no cause for alarm here. Seven years later we know of course that the Global Financial Crisis started in the US, the first modern example of a federation. It spread from there, and that was not the first international catastrophe to emanate from the USA. However, economic problems in a nation can have many other causes than the federal structure. This work by Twomey and Withers was commissioned by the Council for the Australian Federation, which was formed in 2006 by the then all ALP State Premiers who, at that time, apparently felt sympathetic towards such an outcome, possibly after a study visit to Canada. Their vested interests may have been a sleeping motivator as well. Drummond, a co-convener of **Beyond Federation,** has also analysed some of the outcomes of the *Australian 2020 Summit,* convened by Prime Minister Kevin Rudd in his first term. He found that of 790 people who entered submissions to the Governance stream, about 343 contained content that were at least partly relevant to **Beyond Federation** objectives, including about 134 that either explicitly called for the abolition of state governments or called for reforms very close to abolition. However, in contrast, a conference *Making Federalism Work* (ANSZOG 11/12 Sept, 2008) was mainly about that, rescuing federation. A subsequent Conference in Tenterfield, in October 2008, organized by the Federation Research Centre of Griffith University and the Institute of Public Administration Australia (IPAA) was considering Cooperative Federalism. It was attended by many senior public servants, politicians and some academics. My own paper there '*Meliorist piecemeal tinkering with federalism: recipe for disaster?*' offered the view that Cooperative Federalism was no long-term solution for the problem of deteriorating federal-state relations at all.

A recent paper by the late Richard Murray may seem to have been a new departure. It is entitled: New Federation with a Cities and Regional Approach (2012).

Murray was a retired senior economist of Treasury, with experience in the IMF. Much of his paper is devoted to improving fiscal imbalance, as with others before him, e.g. the economist J. Pincus (*Six myths of federal-state financial relations,* CEDA 2007). The Murray proposal has some merit and is more progressive than the one by Pincus who judged the Australian federation as *"the most successful in modern history"*, a view that discourages younger people to tackle the constitutional impasse.

However, what is altogether missing in the papers of Murray and Pincus is a discussion about what the essential characteristics of a federation are, why it is formed, and how the circumstances of the society it serves can change significantly over time. This can be so drastic that maintaining a once useful structure becomes a costly burden. A federation always requires a written constitution and a constitutional court overseeing the division of sovereignty laid down in that constitution. This has been so difficult in Australia that several well known commentators have described the constitution as 'frozen'. To get it out of the deep freeze, piecemeal tinkering and meliorism strategies are certain to fail. Yet, it seems extremely difficult to exit this mode of operation. Economists and constitutional lawyers approach federalism from a different perspective than political scientists. Federation is essentially a power bargain that is then written up in a constitution. The power relationships change over time, for all kinds of reasons, but the written constitution can drag behind, as it has in Australia, in many areas.

Murray wanted to do away with the states but rejects a unitary state early in the proposal because he equated it with a centralized state. Many unitary states are in fact highly decentralized, organized on the principle of flexible subsidiarity, meaning decentralization to its lowest *effective* level. The notion that federalism ensures effective decentralization is another widely-held misconception. The centralization problem in this country exists primarily at the state level, while growing state financial weakness aggravates that situation.

Still, Murray suggested a 'New Federation' as a 'revamp' of the old one, although it seems quite different in many ways. There would be five major city governments and 19 regional governments, named Regional Councils, and a two-tier structure, national ('new federal') and regional. Here is a statement as to revenue collection.

> **"Revenue powers** would also be clearly divided between the two tiers of government. The Federal Government would have direct constitutional power for raising personal and business income taxes, customs and excise duties, and resource taxes. The City and Regional Councils would be constitutionally empowered to raise consumption taxes, land taxes and congestion taxes under nationally agreed regimes covering these taxes".

Regional Parliaments – Regional Governments?

However, there is not much discussion at all about the detail of regional parliaments and regional governments. Are they essentially smaller versions of the existing states? How large will they be? Will there be regional civil services, and, if so, how appointed? It seems that local government would be abolished as well. The City and Regional Councils would take over the work of the huge number of local councils (564). Authority would be *"delegated"* by the federal government although this is NOT a federal way of doing things. However, local democracy would certainly end as a result, rather than be strengthened and improved.

While rejecting a unitary model Murray doesn't mention the need for constitutionally divided sovereignty in a new type of federation. This is quite contradictory.

A stronger COAG type body would make some sense in a New Federation but who really wants a New Federation of no less than five City Governments and 19 mini-states (called Regions here). And what can be made of this quote?:

> **"ROLE OF THE COUNCIL OF AUSTRALIAN GOVERNMENTS**
>
> *A revamped Constitution on a city and regional basis would bring a fresh start to how we address important economic, social and environmental reforms in the national interest. **Admittedly, under this new, federated structure, power would shift further to the Federal Government***

(emphasis added). With a less balanced power sharing, there would be a need for a fundamental institution in which the two tiers of government could come together to forge a partnership between policy design and legislation (Federal responsibility), and the consequential delivery of programs and services flowing from those policy reforms (city/regional responsibility)."

The notion that cooperation is fundamental to a well functioning federal system is laudable but it requires a completely different party system than Australia's adversarial two-party oligarchy. The combative, aggressive political culture of this country, where opposing parties are in government in different states and at the federal level, has frequently made the existing federation virtually unworkable. Revamps of federalism **cannot** be properly discussed without recognition of this problem.[2] Perhaps the very first step towards restructuring is to change the party system, and that really means replacing the electoral system that so unfairly benefits the two major parties. This is not the place to discuss the many flaws in Australia's hybrid electoral systems. However, the 2010 and 2013 federal elections have again demonstrated that these also cry out for drastic reform. There can be little doubt that these systems have contributed greatly to block opportunities for updating the Australian Constitution.

In addition, and relevant to the lack of decentralization, the single-member-district electoral system has often been a barrier to decentralization except where a district becomes a marginal seat in rural areas. I have witnessed this for some 24 years in the Northern Rivers area of New South Wales. National Party (NP, formerly the Country Party) MPs held almost all state and federal seats when I took up an academic appointment in Lismore in January 1975. National Party MPs are members of a rural conservative party that is generally in solid Coalition alliance with the Liberal Party and its predecessors. The NP is not a 'balance of power' party. This situation changed dramatically in the Northern Rivers area during the period from 1974 to 1990. The impact of the Nimbin Green revolution and the establishment of Southern Cross University changed the voting pattern.

---

2   A further critique of the Murray proposal is contained in Appendix 1 in this book written by our contributor Anthony Nicholas.

The Australian Labor Party gained ground with Green preferences. Most seats there became marginal and as a result, money started to flow to the area. In the 1990 federal election the NP even lost the Richmond seat. Its leader Charles Blunt, who had taken over from the Anthony dynasty, was beaten by ALP candidate Neville Newell who won on the preferences of Dr. Helen Caldicott, the anti-nuclear campaigner (23%). In the two-party system marginal seats mostly determine the outcome of elections. They benefit greatly from pork barreling and government attention. Where rural seats are comfortably held by NP MPs there is no real impetus for decentralization measures that would move people from the large population centres to the regions. Assistance to farmers and their related industries is of course important and both major parties are well aware of this but that in itself does not develop decentralized industries and encourage people away from the metropoles. The single-member-district system, in the main, has kept rural Australia rural and, at the same time, forced the major cities to absorb the huge population increase including the large migrant intake since WWII. Of course, there are historical and other factors that have resulted in a very high concentration of people in major cities, such as the early developments around easily accessible ports and, with migrants, the much better job opportunities in the major cities.

AUSTRALIA'S LARGEST CITIES, JUNE 2011

1	Sydney (NSW)	4,627,345
2	Melbourne (VIC)	4,137,432
3	Brisbane (QLD)	2,074,222
4	Perth (WA)	1,738,807
5	Adelaide (SA)	1,212,982
6	Gold Coast – Tweed (QLD/NSW)	600,475
7	Newcastle (NSW)	552,776
8	Canberra – Queanbeyan (ACT/NSW)	417,860
9	Wollongong (NSW)	293,503
10	Sunshine Coast (QLD)	254,650
11	Hobart (TAS)	216,656

12	Geelong (VIC)	180,805
13	Townsville (QLD)	176,327
14	Cairns (QLD)	153,075
15	Toowoomba (QLD)	132,936
16	Darwin (NT)	128,073
17	Albury – Wodonga (NSW/VIC)	107,086
18	Launceston (TAS)	106,655
19	Ballarat (VIC)	97,810
20	Bendigo (VIC)	92,934
21	Mandurah (WA)	89,559
22	Mackay (QLD)	87,324
23	Burnie – Devonport (TAS)	82,913
24	Latrobe Valley (VIC)	81,572
25	Rockhampton (QLD)	78,643
26	Bunbury (WA)	70,037
27	Bundaberg (QLD)	69,500
28	Hervey Bay (QLD)	61,691
29	Wagga Wagga (NSW)	59,005
30	Coffs Habour (NSW)	53,798
31	Gladstone (QLD)	52,949
32	Mildura (VIC)	50,909
33	Shepparton (VIC)	50,373

Source: Australian Bureau of Statistics: Regional Population Growth, Australia, 2010 – 11 (Cat. No. 3218.0)

As the above table shows, over 15 million live in only eight major cities out of a total population 23 million or about 67%, in this very large country. This pattern is typical of 'third world' nations.

However, it surely has become more obvious that the market cannot fix the huge population imbalance between major cities and regional Australia.

Government intervention and stimulation is essential to give this a start but the major parties have basically given up. What the major parties in the metropoles are concerned with, at the state level, is how they overcome the mounting traffic problems, the congestion, the pollution, the time and petrol wasting in getting people to and from work, the psychological problems associated with all this, the high cost of real estate and rents. There are endless plans and inquiries, great future scenarios but even if they catch up a little that very outcome will keep more people in the cities. The answer is not to create more marginal rural seats but, to change the electoral system altogether, away from the single-member-district system to proportional representation, with multi-member-districts.

Certain aspects of the Westminster system also grossly hinder effective federal government. Amazingly, this is still not recognized by most other theorists who say that they have a plan to 'repair' the federation. Two aspects of the Westminster system in particular play havoc with good governance.

The Westminster system originated in the UK and only exists in that country and in some of the British Commonwealth or former Commonwealth countries. Many of the positive values of that system exist in most indirect democracies but there are at least two major differences. In the Westminster system (a) there is a very limited choice of competent cabinet ministers; (b) there is a fusion between the government and the principal legislature. These problems diminish the quality of both the government and the legislature. There is no reason at all that Australia should have to continue with these negative features. To the extent that there are problems with that, Australians should make adjustments. One would expect political scientists to raise such issues but apart from Professor Robert Manne there seems to be no one else who has done that in the last 30 years. The Westminster System is defined as a representative parliamentary system in which the Ministers are *"in and of the parliament"*. Citizens cannot be ministers unless they are elected to Parliament. This virtually ensures that most Ministers are functional amateurs. In the UK the choice is from 600 MPs, minus the opposition MPs. In Australia's federal parliament it is only 228 Senators and MPs, minus the opposition.

Significantly, Murray stated that the COAG reform agenda *"has stalled".* That was to be expected; it is a growing new public service agency on a mission impossible. To the extent that it streamlines state differences it actually succeeds in making the case for the replacement of federation even stronger.

What this means is that any proposals to find a new form of governance for Australia needs to be based on a **comprehensive** approach. The operations of COAG would have to be redirected from the current 'cooperative federalism' ideology, mistakenly re-introduced by the Rudd Government in the previous term. The answer is: **'search beyond federalism.'** In his chapters three and four Richard Murray's approach to a 'fiscal framework' and 'federal financial relations' actually outlines that the dominant financial power of the national government makes a new federation of five cities and 19 regions basically impractical. It is plainly dangerous to resurrect such a new federal structure. Let us start afresh by calling a spade a spade.

The self-funded group *Beyond Federation* is committed to considering *alternatives* to federation. That is what it has been discussing since 2002: http://www.beyondfederation.org.au/

Galaxy Public Opinion Poll

In February 2013 and in May 2014 the Beyond Federation group engaged a reputable Opinion Pollster (Gallaxy) to test public opinion. In the first test it presented one particular question to a national sample of 1052 Australians aged 18 years and over:

Question:

Thinking now about state and federal laws. Currently there are different laws in the eight states and territories of Australia. Would you be in favour or opposed to having just one set of laws for the whole country?

Three answers were possible: 1. In favour: 2. Opposed: 3. Neither/Don't know.

Main Findings

- The majority of Australians are in favour of having a unified set of laws for all states and territories. Overall, 78% are in favour of having one set of laws, 19% are opposed and 3% are uncommitted.

- This means that those in favour of a single set of laws outnumber those opposed by a factor of four to one.

- Majority support may be observed across all key demographic groups and all states of Australia.

In May 2014 the Gallaxy pollsters put the following questions to a national sample of 1050 people, 18 years and over.

It has been estimated that the abolition of State governments could benefit Australia to the tune of at least $40 billion per annum. If a referendum were held on the question of whether State governments should be abolished, would you support the abolition of State governments?

Yes 1,   No 2,   Don't know 3.

Main Findings

1. Opinion is divided on whether the State governments should be abolished. While 39% of the population think they should be, 31% are opposed and 30% undecided.

2. Although those in favour of abolishing State governments outnumber those opposed, the large number of those undecided and the tendency for voters to prefer to maintain the status quo means that a referendum on the issue would be unlikely to be carried at the present point in time.

3. Those aged 50 years and older (50%) are the most likely to be in favour of the abolition of State governments. In contrast, only 18% of those

aged 18-24 years see a need to abolish State governments, with the majority of these young voters (51%) undecided.

4. Men (46%) are more likely than women (32%) to support the abolition of State governments.

5. These results confirm the need for an education campaign, if the push for the abolition of State governments is to be successful. Key targets for the campaign will include young voters and women.

What IS interesting in Murray's paper is the recognition that the larger cities should occupy a second tier position and therefore have a direct relationship with the national government. The Lord Mayor of Sydney, Ms. Clover Moore, is one who has favoured a more direct relationship with the federal government and issued the following media release on 26th November 2007:

"Election Over - Now Time for Cities-Federal Government Alliance

Sydney is "ready, willing and able" to forge a new bi-lateral agreement with the new Federal Government to jointly pursue increased productivity, greater access to global markets, and to help "future-proof" capital cities. "

Congratulating Kevin Rudd on his election victory, Ms Moore said "the City of Sydney supported the initiative of the Council of Capital City Lord Mayors (CCCLM) for a series of direct agreements between the Federal Government and the capital cities as a means of kick-starting a new investment alliance with Canberra, and a new style of Federalism for a new era."

"We need a new national cities policy and the capital cities have been working together to develop a new relationship with the Federal Government, flowing on from meetings in August with politicians from all sides," Ms Moore said. "The City of Sydney thinks a five year agreement to deal with priority issues of national importance and missing links in our federal system is the right approach."

Note: The Council of Capital City Lord Mayors (CCCLM) set up a secretariat in Canberra in 2005 to develop policy and lobby the Federal Government for action. The comprehensive policy document, Partners in Prosperity, is the outcome of that work. The need for a Federal Capital Cities Policy has the support of the Business Council of Australia, the Committee for Economic Development of Australia, the Productivity Commission, the Property Council of Australia, Engineers Australia and the Planning Institute of Australia.

The historical development of federalism – and its decline – has been predicted correctly by eminent Australia commentators as early as 1902 when Alfred Deakin, the second prime minister, said that the *"Commonwealth would increase in stature, in financial dominance, and in the determination of national priorities".* Professor Gordon Greenwood (1942) later wrote that

> *"Despite its achievements, the evidence points decisively to the conclusion that the federal system has outlived its usefulness, that the conditions which made federation a necessary stage in the evolution of Australian nationhood have largely passed away, and that the retention of the system now operates only as an obstacle to effective government and to a further advance."*

At present the Australian Constitution, as well as the political system, is frozen. Sawer already remarked on this 47 years ago (Sawer, 1967). The refrain of "cooperative federalism" is like hearing an old gramophone record with the needle stuck in the groove.

Twomey and Withers (2007) briefly considered the alternative of abolishing the states and replacing them with a much larger number of regions, but rejected that as *"impractical and costly".* They gave no consideration to a decentralised unitary model comprising a new national government and stronger local governments, including (metropolitan) city governments. Existing regional organisation of councils could play a more significant role in assisting local government, facilitating improved subsidiarity. There are already 64 in place in Australia, some of them providing excellent services to local governments (e.g. WSROC, the Western Sydney Regional

Organisation of Councils). Also ignored are problems with the electoral systems, the resulting archaic two-party system and the extremely rigid and now ossified Constitution itself. The Business Council of Australia has issued at least two major reports on Federal-State complexities and inefficiencies, e.g. the high number of taxes impacting on business. They estimated the cost of federation to be approximately $9 billion a year (BCA, 2006). Still, the BCA also favours 'cooperative (seamless) federalism'. Are they suggesting that the clock should be turned back? Did they look further than business interests? Did they make a case for stimulating decentralization away from the major cities? Not really.

Drummond (2007) initially put the cost of continued federation at around $30 billion per annum (in 2002 dollars). Most estimates vary from $9 billion to $40 billion. It could easily be much more simply because future savings are often difficult to quantify. How can one express in dollar terms progress of a national system that is effectively decentralized in which regions and country towns suddenly start to flourish as never before?

Perhaps the most questionable conservative defence is that "a unitary state equals centralization of power". This almost sounds like a remnant of cold war thinking. Surprisingly, the economist Pincus nevertheless points approvingly to France, which is politically highly centralized but administratively effectively decentralized. There are many other examples, which demonstrate that unitary states are often actually more decentralized than federal Australia.

Obviously the final question is: "How can it be changed?" It seems such a difficult, comprehensive transformation to achieve. The barriers to constitutional change appear to be formidable; the two-party system is in the way and there are plenty of vested interest to maintain the status quo. This is where leadership comes in. Of course, the federal government is the unit that needs to take the *bold* initiative. What is involved here is major constitutional change. The onus is on the party or coalition in government at the federal level to formulate a referendum to initiate a mechanism or process resulting in a new constitution proposal.

The Abbott Government appears to be quite conservative on many issues, especially in relation to the environment, women, refugees, the economy, health, education and welfare. Nevertheless, it seems appropriate to quote at some length from Abbott's surprising after-dinner speech delivered at a conference on federalism in Tenterfield, late October, 2008. The conference was held at the Sir Henry Parkes School of Arts Museum and was organized by The Federalism Project of Griffith University and the Institute of Public Administration of Australia. The Conference coincided with the Anniversary of the famous Tenterfield Oration by Sir Henry Parkes, Premier of NSW, on 24th October, 1889. Returning from Queensland he had to change trains at the Wallangarra Railway Station, right on the state border, and was invited to speak at a local reception in nearby Tenterfield. It was there that he called for the political cooperation that led to the first successful Australian federation conference in 1890, and the convention that drafted much of the present federal constitution, in 1891.

Tony Abbott's Speech at Tenterfield

Tony Abbott said on that symbolic occasion in Tenterfield:

> *"I appeal to the distinguished academic political scientists and professional students of government here tonight: don't assume that changing the constitutional position of the states is mission impossible. What's the point of political science faculties if they merely analyse the system rather than help to make it better?*
>
> *The states don't exist because Australia's constitutional founders thought that three levels of government were needed to avoid tyranny. They exist because it was the only way to make a nation out of six colonies. It was the need for a deal that gave us states, not adherence to principle.*
>
> *Take health policy, for instance. Problems in our public hospitals have two basic causes: first, there's not enough money; and second, there's not enough autonomy. The funding problem is hard to resolve because no one government is responsible for it. The management problem is hard to address because every state has a history of micro- managing hospitals from head office. It's almost impossible to tackle these problems without*

addressing the wider issue of federalism. A public hospital controversy invariably provokes a state claim that the quantum of federal funding is inadequate plus a federal counter-claim about poor management and inadequate performance. The government, which runs the hospitals, doesn't fully fund them. The government with the legal responsibility lacks the financial clout and perhaps the political authority to run the service. No-one is really in charge. That is the real problem, which, to a greater or lesser extent, bedevils schools, major infrastructure, disability services, public housing, and environmental management as well as public hospitals.

Should Victoria be able to veto reform of water use in the Murray Darling basin; should NSW be able to opt out of an education revolution; should all the states bar Western Australia be able to stymie a national bid to provide more disability accommodation? I doubt it. Should modern Australia consider itself bound by the intergovernmental arrangements of a previous century, even as adjusted by the High Court; or should matters in dispute be settled by the national parliament as the highest democratic authority in the land? On this, I think we all have a clear sense of where the public really stands."

These remarkable statements from the now Prime Minister, taken directly from his written speech that was made available later, do not even convey the obvious enthusiasm with which it was delivered. Indeed, Mr. Abbott actually said more than what was printed. It was quite obvious to me and others present there that the printed version had been moderated. It was equally amazing that the speaker-in-reply, former ALP Premier of South Australia, John Bannon, defended the existing federal system and pleaded for its continuation.

The now Prime Minister Abbott concluded as follows:

"Of the three options for fixing the federation, mere tinkering, on the grounds that this is about as good as it can get, is really a cop out. Giving more authority and commensurate revenue powers back to the states is possible but implausible. So why not give the national government constitutional authority to match people's expectations about who should

really be in charge? Let's amend section 51 of the Constitution to empower the national parliament to make laws generally for the peace, order and good government of the Commonwealth. This would not abolish the states – just ensure that in the event of disagreement, the national government calls the shots. Change will come, once Kevin Rudd's version of cooperative federalism fails, as it inevitably will, so we'd better all start thinking about the best ways to make it happen."

Such a first step could result in a complete rewrite of the Constitution subsequently but it would have to be accompanied by measures to accommodate the large number of state politicians and state public servants. That would be a boon for local government, a level of government that would be strengthened. Nevertheless, it is in this major area of governance that Tony Abbott appears to have had the potential to make a contribution.

After winning the federal election in September 2013 Abbott seems to have changed his tune considerably, and not for the better. In his Budget proposals additional financial responsibilities were referred back to the States, especially in the health and education areas, and the ultra-conservative refrain of reviving the capacity of the states was heard. The Abbott Government appeared to follow the wish list of the Institute of Public Affairs, an extreme right-wing think tank, which is greatly inspired by the forces of the market place. Opinion polls soon indicated that the Abbott Government had quickly lost the sympathy of the majority of the voters. One would think that if Abbott were to emerge as a significant leader he should follow the direction he expressed in Tenterfield in 2008. Since becoming Opposition leader and then Prime Minister, he has strayed from that path and finds himself surrounded by functionally incompetent ministers in several important policy areas.

Effective decentralization in Australia has not been a concern of either major party for quite a few years, perhaps even decades. At the state level, especially in Sydney and Melbourne, the rapid growth of population in the big cities has resulted in policy directions to best manage the urban sprawl. This has resulted in policies concentrating on increasingly higher density in city areas accompanied by a large range of environmentally negative consequences. Although there may be benefits from higher density in some cases, more especially for developers and investors, there would be many more benefits, for the nation as a whole, flowing from effective decentralization of population growth to the regions.

The mindset of planners in the city is often not suited to that direction and the market place does not see major profits in attempting costly schemes with uncertain outcomes. After the appointment of Ms. Pru Goward, as NSW Coalition Government Planning Minister, the State Coalition Government reinforced its policy direction of higher density for Sydney but now with the sweetener of the compromise that *"nobody would be exempt from the pain involved in this"*. The *"burden would be shared"*, she announced (SMH 31/5/2014). Critics soon responded: *"high-rise should not be imposed on us"*. Chris John, CEO of the NSW Urban Task Force, endorsed this 'necessity' the next day with population statistics that Sydney would grow by 1.5 million over the next 20 years and that increased 'apartment living' was simply inevitable. This kind of discourse again illustrates the abandonment of effective decentralization in Australia, a failure to see the big picture. It is directly related to the dysfunctional relationship between federal and state governments in that the states have become financially too weak to undertake such effective decentralization. This is so because effective decentralization cannot be left to the 'market place fixes all' ideology. It also requires significant public investment, political will and commitment. Currently, that is not forthcoming from either the federal government or the states, perhaps with the exception of marginal seats around election time! What are needed here are incentives to create industries and public services in the regions, through incentives for investors, employers and employees.

At the federal level decentralization has been mooted by plutocrats in relation to economic development in the Northern Territory – more especially as a 'special economic zone' where, presumably, low wages would attract new immigrants, the unemployed and investors. The idea has merit of course but not on the basis of low wages. Decentralisation should be the principal policy direction of the twenty-first century. This would unburden the population pressure in the big cities, an obviously sensible goal. The one success story of the last few decades has been the new regional universities, creating a range of subsidiary services locally. It can be done. Effective, environmentally responsible decentralisation surely is an extremely important objective for this huge continent. It requires a strong and determined national government to achieve that, everywhere.

Chapter 2

Australian Constitution lacks spirit, so tinkering will not help anyone

Justin Smith

Adam Goodes has been named Australian of the Year. A pleasing choice. A top sportsman who showed cool courage when handling the racism of an overzealous young fan last year.

Anti-Australia Day Graffiti attacks at Botany Bay and on Captain Cook's cottage in Melbourne's Fitzroy Gardens made some news last week, then rolled off like muddy water on a red, white and blue duck.

But then Tony Abbott announced his plans to change the constitution of Australia. By September, the Prime Minister would like a draft copy of a new preamble - one that recognises the Aboriginal people as the first Australians.

At first it seems like a strong and symbolic brick for the house of reconciliation, but think about it and you realise this is a total waste of time.

Most of us wouldn't know the contents of the constitution from a lame joke inside a Christmas bonbon, or the back cover of a Stephen King novel. We know of it, we just don't know what's in it.

It's not stupidity; nor ignorance. And it's not our fault. It's just simply so dull it has never warranted the emotional attention or the patriotic inspiration of Australians.

We can all remember those books we would rush home to read - hiding under the blankets with a torch, staying up late to be chilled and thrilled by words. This would never happen with the constitution. Only people with an academic gun to their heads can make it through.

But one thing does make it interesting - just how much is missing from the document.

The prime minister - the most powerful political figure and the head of the government - is not mentioned, and the cabinet - that group of pushy climbers - is not in there. But the governor-general is there. Big time. Most people think the G-G is there to deal with a ribbon in need of a cut, and to grab a hand if it needs a shake. It's a smiling job of ceremony and salutes.

But have a read of the constitution. The governor-general gets to appoint everyone, sack everyone, and move around the defence forces like toy soldiers. Chapter II, section 68: "The command in chief of the naval and military forces of the Commonwealth is vested in the governor-general as the Queen's representative."

If you think we had a constitutional crisis in 1975, wait until a PM orders troops overseas and the G-G orders them back again. It will read like a David Williamson play ...

PM: You can't do that. I'm the Prime Minister!

GG: (holding up large copy of the constitution) Well, I don't see your name in here anywhere, mate.

Yes, there are plenty of bits, sections and words to protect the states, and there are legal crumbs to help us argue a case to the High Court. But the words give us nothing to boast about or inspire us.

The Americans seem to have an endless loop of patriotic choruses to sew together and jabber when needed. This is self-evident. And the British can chant about their "mountains green" to great sporting effect. Even when they lose.

Our constitution gives us none of this. So changing, fiddling, reworking or adding to it is unlikely to advance the process of reconciliation and understanding.

It's a shame, because it would be wonderful if it could. The people of a beautiful and ancient race are in trouble. They have been for some years. In the timeline of their long history, this is not a glorious period.

Words are important. They can hurt and can be glorious. People like Nelson Mandela have used the right ones in the right places to lift the world and disarm enemies. Words have an impact on health, life expectancy, unemployment, tension, awareness, failings and hopes.

But they need to be read and heard first. Maybe they're in the words we use every day.

Justin Smith hosts *Drive* on 2UE 954.

This article is republished from the Sydney Morning Herald, January 29th, 2014.

Read more: http://www.smh.com.au/comment/australian-constitution-lacks-spirit-so-tinkering-will-not-help-anyone-20140128-31kr2.html#ixzz2wBYu3WfS

Chapter 3

The shortcomings of the Australian Constitution

Klaas Woldring

Although the existing Constitution is mostly seen as quite an achievement in 1901, it now presents a set of ground rules that are antiquated and often dysfunctional. To the extent they are useful they could easily be incorporated in a new Constitution. Trying to amend and update the 1901 Constitution has proved to be virtually impossible. Since WWII the major parties have avoided essential amendments or have ingeniously circumvented the Constitution, or "creative" High Court decisions have provided solutions. As Law Professor Cheryl Saunders has remarked, "there is of course a limit to how today's judges can creatively imply what the 'founding fathers' in the late 1890s may have meant with clauses relevant at that time".

In addition, the "new-found constitutional protection for political communication" (an implied right) is seen as a value, which underpins parliamentary responsible government. But, she wrote, "there are limits to what courts can do in interpreting an old Constitution, e.g. "Judges cannot find human rights and liberties in there which simply aren't there, try as they may".

Surely it is important the Constitution reflects the values, ways and ambitions of contemporary society. What society would allow it to be governed from the grave, especially one that has changed as much as Australian society in the last 114 years? This Constitution is not a set of historic fundamental laws such as govern the UK – which has no written constitution otherwise – a highly exceptional case. We are a de facto independent country, a federation with a written Constitution dividing powers and functions between the constituent units that have changed dramatically in those 114 years. Continued ineffectual piecemeal tinkering is no solution, to the contrary.

It is therefore very surprising that no major political party has adopted a conscious and well formulated policy for constitutional system change. One would think such a policy could create considerable electoral support especially if developed together with educational programs and participation by voters in the process. This is a problem in itself of course: lack of public participation, especially by the young who, with the important exception of the Internet, have abandoned discourse about constitutional and political issues.

The Constitutional Commission of 1986 – 1988.

A serious attempt to review the Constitution was actually made by this Commission. Its members were: Sir Maurice Byers QC, Professor Enid Campbell, Hon. Sir Rupert Hamer, Hon. Justice John Toohey, Hon. E. G. Whitlam, QC and Professor Leslie Zines. The Commission was assisted by a number of expert advisory committees:

- Executive government

- Distribution of powers

- Trade and national economic management

- Individual and democratic rights under the Constitution

- The Australian judicial system

This is not the place to examine in detail what ground was covered.

It can be said that it was a fairly extensive examination and that the need for it was not in doubt whatever. Economic management, distribution of powers and human rights were given much attention and quite detailed recommendations followed. In the end the question of what could be put to the people in a Referendum as a first serious attempt to "update" the Constitution, with some hope of success, was a vexed question. Considerable debate occurred as to the legal capacity to change the Constitution altogether, outside Section 128, as the Constitution was still "encased" in British constitutional law and practices. The role of the Australia Act (s) of 1986 gave rise to much discussion among constitutional lawyers but it was inconclusive. The following four questions were finally put to the voters:

1. *Constitution Alteration (Parliamentary Terms) 1988* proposed to alter the Australian constitution such that Senate terms be reduced from six to four years, and House of Representative terms be increased from three years to four years. It also proposed for the fourth time that Senate and House elections occur simultaneously.

2. *Constitution Alteration (Fair Elections) 1988* proposed to enshrine in the constitution a guarantee that all Commonwealth, State and Territory elections would be conducted democratically.

3. *Constitution Alteration (Local Government) 1988* proposed to alter the constitution so as to recognise local government.

4. The *Constitution Alteration (Rights and Freedoms) 1988* was proposed legislation that was put to referendum in the **Australian Referendum, 1988**. The legislation sought to enshrine in the Australian Constitution various civil rights, including freedom of religion, rights in relation to trials, and rights regarding the compulsory acquisition of property.

Initially, three of the proposals, put by the Hawke Government, had tentative bi-party support for these proposals, but this was withdrawn altogether during the campaign. In the end the Coalition parties opposed all four proposals. The highest national vote was 37.6 % for the "Fair Elections" question. Once again it was demonstrated that constitutional referenda fail unless they have support from both major parties. The major parties basically gave up for the next 26 years. Before that the only successful referendum was in 1977.

However, following this failure a number of academics and a few political journalists started making various cases for rewriting the Constitution altogether, including the author of this chapter (APSA *Newsletter* 66/1993).

Journalist David Solomon, as well as academics Helen Irving and George Williams attempted to move away from piecemeal tinkering. Solomon, in his 1999 book *Coming of Age*, called for the radical overhaul of the Australian Constitution in order to achieve an effective Republic. Here is a small part of an extensive review by journalist Tony Stephens.

> *"Solomon's proposals would bring major changes to Australia's version of the Westminster system of government, reviving the doctrine of separation of powers between parliament, government and the judiciary, and restoring power to the people. They include:*

- A parliament of only one house that would have primary law-making powers

- Ministers would be selected on merit, from outside parliament, to form the government

- A bill of rights would protect peoples' rights and freedoms

> *Solomon comprehensively rejects the conservative guidelines 'if it ain't broke, don't fix it'. He argues that Australia's system is in "desperate need of repair and must be fixed if Australia is to prosper". The most radical of the suggested changes is that "the (directly elected) President should have powers similar to the US President". This 1999 book was published too late to have a major impact though - one month before the Referendum.*

Helen Irving, a constitutional historian (UTS and Sydney University) devoted the 2001 Barton Lecture to the constitutional issue.

> *"The (1901) Constitution was written in response to a wide range of interests and wishes. People knew and understood the debates, and when they looked at the completed product, they saw in it almost nothing that they did not recognise. This is not the case today. The Constitution is probably unintelligible to most Australians in 2001. I don't mean*

unintelligible because the vast majority has never seen it, let alone read it. I mean, even if they had seen it - indeed, particularly if they had seen it. .... Australia's relations with Britain have undergone many changes since 1901, and a range of sections, which refer to the old imperial ties, are no longer operative. The Empire—once a great and familiar idea to Australians - is scarcely remembered, let alone understood.... many of the institutions created and authorised by the Constitution are described in confusing and even misleading ways. What they do say depends upon a body of unwritten conventions and lies largely 'between the lines... many of the issues of the 19th century are not the issues of today.'"

George Williams (2002), a well-known UNSW Law Professor, provided five reasons to rewrite the Constitution:

1. The Constitution is out of touch with political reality. He argues that the people know very little about their Constitution, that "it was not written as a people's Constitution but instead as a compact between the Australian colonies to meet the needs of trade and commerce, among other things". So, for instance, it says very little about what it is to be Australian ...how we should behave towards each other as human beings and as Australians". The text of the Constitution does not match political reality because it is premised upon an understanding of the Westminster system of government operating in the United Kingdom".

2. The Constitution has failed the Australian Indigenous peoples. They played no part in the drafting of it and, when it came into force, explicitly discriminated against them, section 51 (26). They are in fact regarded as "outsiders". Reconciliation cannot be successful unless this is rectified.

3. The Constitution doesn't serve the economy well. Although High Court interpretation has enabled the federal parliament to control and regulate the national economy, the federal vision contained in the Australian Constitution is now inconsistent with modern understandings of the Australian economy. Williams writes, "our economy does not consist of discrete and insular

sectors of commerce within each state or even within Australia" (the implication of Section 92 which says that trade, commerce and intercourse among the states shall be absolutely free). In reality it exists within a world of global markets ..."In order to compete effectively on a global scale, given our small population and geographical location, Australia requires national laws on issues ranging from industrial relations to consumer protection and trade practices".

4. The Constitution is almost totally deficient in the areas of social justice and human rights. Williams places great emphasis on this deficiency. That is understandable because many other shortcomings can be challenged from this very perspective. The framers of the Constitution chose to rely on the operation of the Common Law but it is now quite widely accepted that this is indeed very inadequate now.

5. The text of the Constitution suggests that Australia is not an independent nation, argues Williams. This is beyond dispute. Section 2 in particular makes it clear that the Queen is the Head of State and the Governor-General is the Queen's representative. This is the very opposite of an independent Republic. The symbols provided by this Constitution are those of a Monarchy of another country of which Australia is a sub-ordinate overseas Dominion.

Several other academics and writers have added significant contributions to the idea that major changes are required. Patmore, G. & Jungwirth, G. (2000) edited a series of "Labour Essays" entitled *The Big Makeover – a new Australian Constitution*, Pluto Press, which included the Chapter by Williams. In 2004 Hudson, W. and Brown, A. J., scholars of Griffith University, edited *Restructuring Australia – Regionalism, Republicanism and Reform of the Nation-State*, Federation Press, which contains contrasting chapters by those advocating major changes as well others defending the status quo or favouring minimal change. The books by Harris, B. (2002) *A New Constitution for Australia*, Ashgate-Gower Asia Pacific; Winterton, G. (2001) - *Republic Resurrected*, The Federation Press, and Saunders, C.

(2003) (2nd ed) – *It's Your Constitution – Governing Australia Today*, The Federation Press, should also be mentioned; and Ward, A. "Trapped in a Constitution: The Australian Republic Debate" (*Australian Journal of Political Science*, Vol. 35, No. 1, pp. 117-123).

There are many other constitutional complications. Just a few are summarised here:

Apart from the overriding issues flowing from the archaic federal structure there are several other issues that require solutions:

The Corporations Power: That power is laid down in Section 51. It restricts the Commonwealth power to legislate in respect of matters, which are specifically provided in the Constitution. E.g. the Federal Government only has a power to legislate in respect of FOREIGN corporations. This means that the power to deal with national corporations is vested in the states - obviously a serious limitation for the national government. In order to overcome/bypass this problem the National Scheme laws have been enacted in 1989/90. There are four laws that govern this system. There have been complications with this system that many corporate leaders want sorted out - principally by making the Corporate Power a federal concern altogether.

(Source: Andrew Taylor, "From Wakim to Hughes", *Law Society Journal of Western Australia*, October 2000).

Income tax: Since WWII Collection of Income Tax (the main source of revenue for Governments) has been centralised, first as a temporary measure but subsequently it became a permanent feature. Howard Government has tried to put the clock back by handing the GST revenue to the states. Is this the way to go?

Tertiary education: Financed and policy determination by the Federal Government. However organisation, legislation, governance, etc. is a concern of State Governments. Does this make sense?

Expenditure on health: Divided between Commonwealth and States resulting in endless squabbles and inadequacies, e.g. hospital funding.

Investment: Most states have independent investment strategies, promotion and offices (permanent trade commissioners, Premiers making extensive and expensive tours to sell their states). They are looking for and encouraging foreign investors. The foreign investors naturally exploit this inter-state competition and end up with, usually, exceptionally good deals - at the expense of Australia as a whole. Is this what a small nation of 23 million can afford to do?

Distribution of Goods and Services Tax (GST) to states: Has increased the dependency of the states on the Commonwealth (see federal-state issues section in this text). In recent months the quite unequal distribution of GST income amongst the states has caused much concern. This issue has received new attention as revenues of the Federal government are falling short of budgetary requirements.

The lack of human rights guarantees and Indigenous recognition: This was partly overcome by the Racial Discrimination Act, 1977. Amazingly, the current Abbott government initially moved to change this Act by changing Clause 18c in a way that would make the expression of bigotry legal. While this plan has run into considerable opposition, even within the Liberal Party itself, the existence of constitutionally guaranteed human rights and Indigenous recognition, dignity and equality would have made such an objective virtually impossible.

In summary: The Constitution

1. describes a status of dependency on Britain, a situation that for all practical purposes ended after WWII in 1945. The formal position of the Governor-General is that of Her Majesty's powerful principal servant - essentially a colonial relationship. The position of Prime Minister is not even mentioned. Amazingly, decisions on committing the country to a war are left to this Prime Minister. There is no

requirement for parliamentary approval or even discussion, or any participation by the people in the form of a plebiscite or referendum.

2. made provision for a federation, a structure of state, which made good sense in 1900 but is now a costly hindrance to effective government for a mere 23 million people. Local Government is not even mentioned in this Constitution. It has no formal relationship to the national government.

3. hardly mentions the existence of political parties - the reality of the political system. As a result of the single-district electoral system, which exists separate from the Constitution, an inefficient two-party system has developed.

4. has no Bill of Rights, so Australia is the only Commonwealth country that has no such statutory protection of the rights of its citizens.

5. makes no provision for the reconciliation with and representation of the Indigenous Peoples. Recent moves to address this situation have come to nothing thus far.

6. makes no provision for the protection of the environment, a most important new value, which needs to be expressed and safeguarded.

7. makes no provision for the election of a diversity of representatives to the two Houses of Parliament, nationally and in the states. It hardly reflects a multicultural society.

8. makes no provision for the appointment of Cabinet Ministers from outside the legislature, as is the case in most European countries and in the United States. As a result Governments are frequently lacking in quality and expertise.

9. does NOT state that the Government derives its authority from the people's sovereignty - the very essence of democracy - and that of a Republic.

10. does not elaborate on the nature of popular and national sovereignty and does not provide guidance as to how, for instance, economic sovereignty is to be safeguarded and promoted in a globalised world.

11. is embedded in several constitutional conventions (usages), which are open to a variety of interpretations. Conventions should ALL be codified for them to be widely accepted.

12. parliamentary democracy, often praised in Australia as a positive constitutional feature, is in fact NOT protected in the Constitution.

13. the position of women and the issues of equality between the sexes and of gender in Australian society is not addressed anywhere in the Constitution.

14. very few people are familiar with the Constitution. Most who study it find it a seriously flawed, archaic document and don't understand why we still have it. Most people have no sense of ownership of it.

15. it is practically impossible to amend the Constitution, due to the provisions of Section 128 AND the two-party system.

16. many leaders in the corporate sector of Australia are rightly very disenchanted with this Constitution. The Corporation Power in Section 51 is, in practice, used mainly in respect of foreign corporations (with a few exceptions). The states regulate corporate affairs, with sometimes major differences between them, a costly and frustrating situation.

17. *"Neither the Constitution nor the Commonwealth Electoral Act, 1918 nor the electoral Act of 1924 provide for democratic elections – a century of delusion".* This is the title of an article by Dr. Anthony Gray, S.L. in Law, USC. "the Constitution provides no express guarantee of a universal franchise," he claims.

Recent assessments

The resort by the Rudd Government to "cooperative federalism", in 2007, can now only be seen as an opportunity lost. The substantial injection of funds and staff into the Council of Australian Governments (COAG) was understandable in the absence of the ALP's lack of policy on a new Constitution but, six years on, the basic problem remains. While COAG struck a new deal, in 2008, for federal-state financial relations, seen as a positive agreement, this can be undone by any future government. George Williams (2012) writes

"While COAG is the right body for reaching agreement between governments, it does not have the power to entrench those decisions against political opportunism, nor the capacity to bring about deeper structural reform.....Even where COAG works its way around constitutional impediments this may not amount to a long-term solution" (*Tomorrow's Federation*, Ch. 16 "Rewriting the Federation through Referendum").

Williams, one of Australia's leading constitutional lawyers, who appears not to be in favour of replacing federation, does pose this vital question: What can we learn from Australia's past that might inform a better, future referendum strategy? Can we do without constitutional referendums? he asked. The answer is NO. "Some federal reforms can only be achieved by way of a referendum. For these changes there is no substitute process". Frankly, the tone of his chapter is one of near desperation. Indeed, the several other contributors to *Tomorrow's Federation* write about and discuss research within the existing framework, however flawed constitutionally. The real answer is in this eBook. Australia needs a new Constitution. Of course, a sovereign people has the democratic right to rewrite its now archaic Constitution. If the general public begins to understand this and put pressure on the political parties to get their act together, a new draft Constitution can be put before them in terms of Section 128 and this problem will be solved.

If it cannot be amended – rewrite it!

The three often quoted reasons why amendment is virtually impossible are:

Section 128, prescribing the constitutional amendment procedure, requires a triple majority for a referendum to be carried. That formidable barrier is inherent in the federal structure.

Secondly, the exclusive right of initiative to generate a constitutional amendment lies exclusively with the politicians in Australia.

Thirdly, the least mentioned, but very important barrier: the adversarial two-party system, a product of Australia's electoral systems.

But really there is still more. It is the lack of political will in the major political parties who spend an inordinate amount of time rubbishing each other over often trivial and even cooked up issues and differences. They appear incompetent to address the antiquated ground rules of this society. How can it be that such ideas of constitutional renewal do not emerge in the major political parties? Why is it so? Indeed as Alan Ward wrote: they are "Trapped in a frozen Constitution". The time has come for a group of enlightened politicians and academics to write up a proposal for a new Constitution. These people certainly exist but have to come forward. Australia has to move on and forget about any other further referendums to amend this Constitution. The foundations of this constitutional house are crumbling. Further tinkering with the superstructure, if at all possible, is the wrong investment of energy and funds.

Chapter 4

Numerical Perspectives in Support of the Abolition of State Governments

Mark Drummond

This paper briefly examines two interconnected sets of numerical perspectives which strongly support the cause to reform Australia's Federation by abolishing State governments along the lines envisaged by the Australia United Plan (see Appendix II of this book, pages 163-6), albeit a delayed version of that plan, conceding that, as things currently stand in 2014, an Australia without State governments is unlikely to be achieved by the year 2020. The first set of numerical perspectives are survey results from two Galaxy polls commissioned by Beyond Federation and carried out in February 2013 and May 2014 which lay bare the clear cut reality that abolishing State governments is certainly achievable in the medium to long term future, in view of the strong underlying support for a single set of laws across the whole of Australia and the abolition of State governments generally. These survey results make it equally clear, however, that the abolition of Australia's State governments is far from inevitable and will continue to prove very difficult to achieve. The second set of numerical perspectives explores improvements to Australia that could be achieved if an extra $40 billion per annum became available. This second set of perspectives relates to estimates that abolishing State governments can achieve huge financial benefits for Australia, in the order of $20 billion per annum across the public sector alone, and $50 billion per annum across public and private sectors and the entire economy overall (see Drummond 2002; 2007), amounting to about four per cent of Australia's Gross Domestic Product (GDP).

The two sets of numerical perspectives presented herein are interconnected through the wording of the 2014 Galaxy poll survey question, as follows, and by coincidence, the $40 billion figure in this question aligned with Commonwealth government budget shortfalls widely reported in the media following the release of the 2014 Budget on 13 May 2014:

It has been estimated that the abolition of State governments could benefit Australia to the tune of at least $40 billion per annum. If a referendum were held on the question of whether State governments should be abolished, would you support the abolition of State governments?

The estimates, as above, that abolishing State governments can achieve financial benefits for Australia in the order of $20 billion per annum across the public sector alone, and $50 billion per annum across public and private sectors and the entire economy overall, are derived and explained in previous works (Drummond 2002; 2007). In short, these estimates describe the savings and financial benefits generally that could be achieved if Australia moved to a carefully designed, less constrained, system of government comprising just national and local governments (where "local" can also mean "regional" as generally understood), and a single set of laws, thereby eliminating or at least drastically reducing the costs of duplication, coordination, regulation, political border and boundary effects, and other financial and economic impediments, hence enabling improved financial and economic performance by Australia's public and private sectors and economy and society overall, less held back by red tape, excessive taxation and cost of government burdens generally.

February 2013 Galaxy Survey on Levels of Support for One Set of Laws Australia-wide

On the weekend of 1-3 February 2013, Galaxy Research carried out a telephone survey and study, commissioned by Beyond Federation, of a sample of 1052 Australians, using the question and response options as follows below:

Thinking now about state and federal laws. Currently there are different laws in the eight states and territories of Australia. Would you be in favour or opposed to having just one set of laws for the whole country?

Response options:
In favour
Opposed
Neither/ Don't know

The *Australian Laws Study*, Galaxy Research's detailed report of the results of this telephone survey, shows that:

The majority of Australians are in favour of having a unified set of laws for all states and territories. Overall, 78% are in favour of having one set of laws, 19% are opposed and 3% are uncommitted.

This 78% support figure is the Australia-wide figure for all people surveyed. Among females, the Australia-wide support figure is 80%, and for males it is 76%. Sub-national support rates and the Australia-wide figures are summarised in Table 1 below.

Table 1: Support for Just One Set of Laws for the Whole of Australia in February 2013

Parts of Australia	In Favour	Opposed	Neither / Don't Know
New South Wales (including the ACT)	83%	14%	3%
Victoria and Tasmania (combined)	77%	20%	3%
Queensland	80%	17%	2%
South Australia	74%	23%	3%
Western Australia	63%	35%	2%
Whole of Australia	78%	19%	3%
As above but excluding "Neither / Don't Know" responses			
New South Wales (including the ACT)	86%	14%	
Victoria and Tasmania (combined)	80%	20%	
Queensland	82%	18%	
South Australia	76%	24%	
Western Australia	64%	36%	
Whole of Australia	81%	19%	

May 2014 Galaxy Survey on Levels of Support for the Abolition of State Governments

Between Wednesday 14 May and Friday 16 May 2014, Galaxy Research carried out an online survey and study, again commissioned by Beyond Federation, of a sample of 1050 Australian adults, using the question and response options as follows:

> It has been estimated that the abolition of State governments could benefit Australia to the tune of at least $40 billion per annum. If a referendum were held on the question of whether State governments should be abolished, would you support the abolition of State governments?

> Response options:
> Yes
> No
> Don't know

The *State Government Study*, Galaxy's detailed report of the results of this online survey, shows that:

> Opinion is divided on whether the State governments should be abolished. While 39% of the population think they should be, 31% are opposed and 30% undecided.

So excluding the 30% undecided ("Don't know") response, 56% of the population think State governments should be abolished, and 44% are opposed to the abolition of State governments. These 39% (overall) and 56% (excluding "Don't know" undecided responses) support figures are the Australia-wide figures for all people surveyed. Among females, the Australia-wide support figures are just 32% overall and 49% excluding undecided responses, and for males they are 46% overall and 63% excluding undecided responses. Sub-national support rates and the Australia-wide figures are summarised in Table 2 below.

Table 2: Support for the Abolition of State Governments in May 2014

Parts of Australia	In Favour	Opposed	Don't Know
New South Wales (including the ACT)	41%	29%	29%
Victoria and Tasmania (combined)	39%	31%	30%
Queensland	43%	29%	28%
South Australia	31%	34%	35%
Western Australia	30%	36%	22%
Whole of Australia	39%	31%	30%
As above but excluding "Don't Know" responses			
New South Wales (including the ACT)	59%	41%	
Victoria and Tasmania (combined)	56%	44%	
Queensland	60%	40%	
South Australia	48%	52%	
Western Australia	45%	55%	
Whole of Australia	56%	44%	

Figure 1 below summarises the results shown in Tables 1 and 2 above excluding "Neither / Don't Know" responses, with the 1999 Republic Referendum results provided as well as a benchmark for comparative purposes.

Figure 1: Percentage Support for a Republic, Uniform National Laws, and Abolition of State Governments

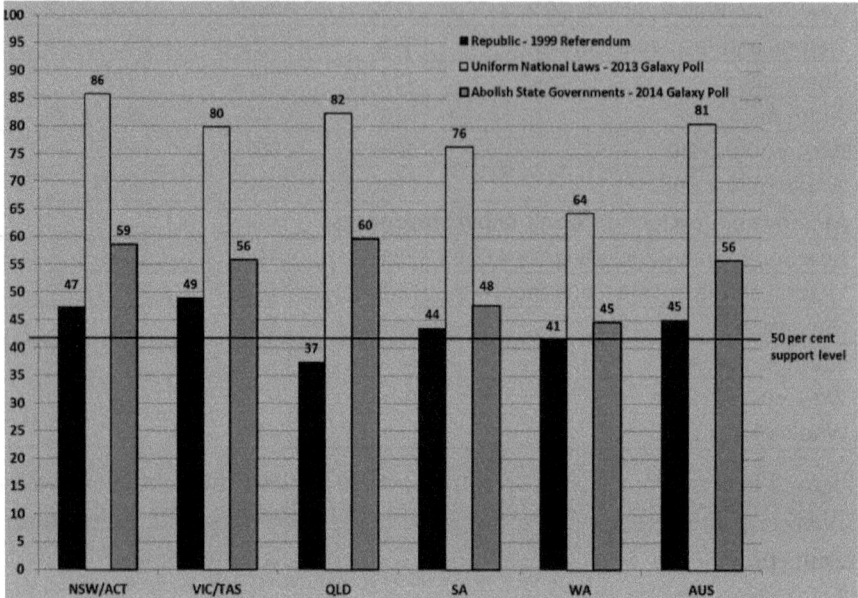

Figure 1: Percentage Support for a Republic, Uniform National Laws, and Abolition of State Governments

Legend:
- Republic - 1999 Referendum
- Uniform National Laws - 2013 Galaxy Poll
- Abolish State Governments - 2014 Galaxy Poll

Values by region:
- NSW/ACT: 47, 86, 59
- VIC/TAS: 49, 80, 56
- QLD: 37, 82, 60
- SA: 44, 76, 48
- WA: 41, 64, 45
- AUS: 45, 81, 56

50 per cent support level

Results here show that Australians very strongly support a move to just one set of laws for the whole of Australia, and whilst there's not yet a dominant majority in support of the abolition of State governments sufficient to carry a Referendum on the question, there is clearly a significant baseline level of support for State government abolition which completely dispels theories and claims that abolishing State governments is impossible or something only supported by an insignificant minority or by unrealistic dreamers. There is clear evidence on display herein and elsewhere that support for State government abolition is at least as strong as support for an Australian Republic, and probably stronger. As has been the case throughout nearly all of Australia's post-Federation history since 1901, the abolition of State governments is a mainstream reform cause with widespread support and realistic hopes of success within decades if not years.

Survey results presented here suggest that a Referendum on the question of whether Australia should have just one set of laws for the whole country would carry very comfortably, and if such a Referendum did carry, and

Australia's Commonwealth, State and Territory governments responded in line with voters' Referendum wishes to produce a single set of laws for Australia-wide operation, then Australia, by the end of that legal unification process, would for all practical purposes no longer have a truly federalist system of government, clearly being unitary from a legal viewpoint. And if that level of national unification was achieved, the abolition of State governments would clearly be vastly more achievable than it is now.

So What Could $40 billion a Year Do for Australia?

The wording of the May 2014 Galaxy survey described earlier in this paper, including the $40 billion figure therein, was confirmed prior to the release of the Commonwealth Government budget on 13 May 2014, and, by extraordinary coincidence, there were numerous media reports soon after the Commonwealth budget was announced about $40 billion worth of severe budget cuts deemed necessary by the Coalition government to overcome the budget deficit. There have also been many other media reports of a "$40 billion budget black hole" and other similarly worded expressions of concerns about budget deficits, funding shortages and funding reductions amounting to $40 billion or similar figures over recent years.

If it is true or at least plausible that several tens of billions of dollars' worth of benefits could be achieved for Australia and Australians if Australia's State and Territory governments were abolished, and their assets and functions transferred to Commonwealth and local governments, then it is well worth contemplating the question of what $40 billion a year, say, could do for Australia. To answer this question, government expenses across all levels of government for the financial year 2012-13, as presented in the Australian Bureau of Statistics publication on Government Finance Statistics (Catalogue 5512.0, released 28 May 2014), provide very helpful insights on the scales of expenditure across different purpose areas, as shown in Table 3 below (adapted from a Table 4 in this Catalogue 5512.0), where the "Total" figures in the rightmost column include local government expenses.

Table 3: General Government Expenses by Purpose in 2012-13 ($m)

Purpose Area	Cwth	NSW	Vic	Qld	SA	WA	Tas	NT	ACT	Total	$40b divided by Total
General public services	22,197	2,413	995	1,666	321	411	228	117	459	33,532	1.19
Defence	20,728	–	–	–	–	–	–	–	–	20,728	1.93
Public order and safety	3,924	6,396	5,138	3,968	1,516	2,940	444	618	387	25,622	1.56
Education	29,334	16,004	12,763	10,509	4,086	6,154	1,254	982	936	79,563	0.50
Primary and secondary	13,771	11,753	9,032	8,339	3,272	4,955	1,001	750	743	40,625	0.98
University	9,248	66	139	1	8	17	–	22	17	22,257	1.80
Technical and further education	2,068	1,807	2,510	783	505	618	166	92	103	6,776	5.90
Health	61,115	16,835	13,052	12,350	5,086	6,903	1,484	1,161	1,229	102,096	0.39
Acute care institutions	2,555	12,082	8,811	7,247	4,396	4,650	1,030	763	930	39,592	1.01
Pharmaceutical	9,832	1,351	36	–	13	531	1	36	25	11,821	3.38
Social security and welfare	131,687	4,907	3,865	2,656	1,152	1,787	379	340	228	146,310	0.27
Housing and community amenities	8,200	2,138	2,345	1,647	1,078	1,534	185	573	155	21,847	1.83
Recreation and culture	3,622	1,348	837	950	386	764	195	193	184	13,012	3.07
Fuel and energy	5,966	29	–	681	53	543	1	111	27	7,397	5.41
Agriculture, forestry and fishing	2,266	731	498	606	155	376	104	70	6	4,311	9.28
Mining, manufacturing and construction	2,920	194	–	426	60	191	12	24	18	4,249	9.41
Transport and communications	5,604	7,582	5,492	6,423	1,013	1,929	275	243	289	29,596	1.35
Other economic affairs	10,702	1,080	851	628	230	719	117	140	59	15,499	2.58
Nominal interest on superannuation	6,729	−161	446	743	314	369	178	114	264	8,996	4.45
Public debt transactions	12,898	2,203	1,775	1,952	388	442	14	184	128	20,647	1.94
Other	55,074	1,557	236	925	133	158	164	15	98	4,381	9.13
Total	382,966	63,255	48,293	46,131	15,972	25,221	5,034	4,885	4,468	537,787	0.07

Source: Australian Bureau of Statistics, 'Government Finance Statistics, Australia, 2012-13' (Catalogue 5512.0, released 28 May 2014)

The above table shows that $40 billion per annum in current dollar terms around the year 2014 or 2013, could fund:

- almost TWO of our annual **Defence** budgets [$20.7b spent in 2012-13]

- more than ONE AND A HALF lots of the entire **Public Order and Safety** system. including all our police forces and courts [$25.6b spent in 2012-13]

- half of all **Education** system spending [$79.6b spent in 2012-3]

- almost the entire **primary and secondary school systems** (the government funded part thereof, so that's the entire public system plus government funding of non-government schools) [$40.6b spent in 2012-13]

- almost TWO of our **University** system budgets [$22.3b spent in 2012-13]

- nearly SIX lots of nationwide **TAFE** funding [$6.8b spent in 2012-13]

- the entire acute care part of the **Health system** (again the government funded part thereof, so the entire public hospital system plus government funding of non-government hospitals) [$39.6b spent in 2012-13]

- more than THREE lots of total spending on **Pharmaceuticals** [$11.8b spent in 2012-13]

- almost TWO of our annual **Housing and community amenities** budgets [$21.8b spent in 2012-13]

- THREE lots of all **Recreation and Culture** spending [$13.0b spent in 2012-13]

- more than FIVE lots of all spending on **Fuel and Energy** [$7.4b spent in 2012-13]

- more than NINE lots of all spending on **Agriculture, Forestry and Fishing** [$4.3b spent in 2012-13]

- more than NINE lots of all spending on **Mining, Manufacturing and Construction** [$4.2b spent in 2012-13]

- ONE AND A THIRD lots of all spending on **Transport and Communications** [$29.6b spent in 2012-13]

- and the list goes on.

In the past few years there have been numerous media reports on the pain suffered by universities undertaking restructures and program rationalisations to make ends meet. Boy oh boy it's galling that universities feel they need to save a few million dollars here and a few hundred thousand there, when there's dozens of billions of dollars worth of duplicated bureaucracy strangling Australia, impeding it's people, it's creativity, and it's enterprise.

On the 25th of August 2014, the front page of the *Canberra Times* newspaper hosted an article by Ross Peake titled 'War memorial ends travelling exhibitions due to shock DVA funding cut'. Quoting Australian War Memorial Director Dr Brendan Nelson, this article states that (quoting the longer online version of the article):

> "After 17 years of its co-sponsorship, the Department of Veterans' Affairs informed the memorial last week that it has found it necessary to cease funding the travelling exhibition program effective immediately. There is no plan for it to be reinstated in the foreseeable future," a statement from the memorial said. The sudden decision comes as the memorial is revamping its World War I galleries and gearing up for commemorations for the centenary of WWI. Dr Nelson said the successful travelling exhibitions program was established about 17 years ago, with exhibitions being displayed in museums and galleries across Australia. "In delivering travelling exhibitions to the Australian public, particularly in regional and rural areas, the memorial has told the story of Australia's military history with support of the memorial's extensive national collection," he said. "The travelling exhibitions program has been delivered through supplementary funding of $800,000 a year from DVA. "The department will certainly not have found this an easy decision, but nonetheless one it could not avoid. "As a result, the memorial must cease the travelling exhibitions program. This will take effect immediately."

So Australia's grossly defective federal system of government effectively wastes in the order of $40 billion a year, and, as a result, numerous meritorious programs like the Australian War Memorial's travelling exhibitions scheme have had to be cut. But if $40 billion a year or so was freed up through the unification – or amalgamation – of Commonwealth, State and Territory governments into a single national government, thereby abolishing State governments, Australia could move to great national systems of education and health, and a great nationwide system of laws, courts and justice, and so on, and thousands of meritorious programs like the Australian War Memorial's travelling exhibitions scheme could so easily be afforded. And surely we'd be better off then than we are now, with under-resourced and all too often underperforming education and health systems, and our nine Commonwealth, State and Territory governments – and local governments also – seemingly always too strapped for cash to fund numerous meritorious programs.

Figure 2 below is a very basic pie chart, intentionally simplistic for illustrative purposes only, that shows how $40 billion dollars a year, that could be liberated if Australia moves beyond its dysfunctional neo-colonial Federation to a well designed unitary system of government with properly empowered national and local governments, could be utilised to address urgent needs called for across the full political spectrum from business lobbyists to green lobbyists to everyone in between and beyond with worthy causes to push.

Figure 2: What $40 billion a Year Could Do for Australia – Two Modest Proposals

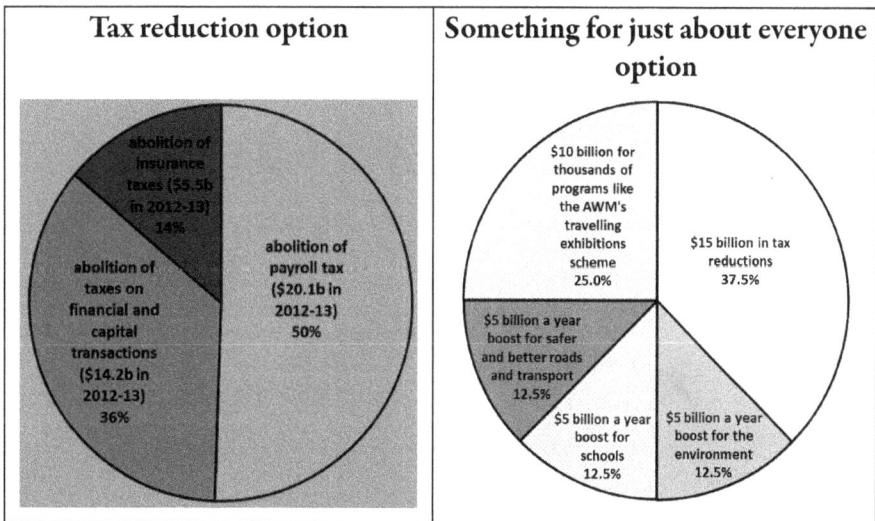

Tax reduction option	Something for just about everyone option

Tax reduction option:
- abolition of insurance taxes ($5.5b in 2012-13) 14%
- abolition of taxes on financial and capital transactions ($14.2b in 2012-13) 36%
- abolition of payroll tax ($20.1b in 2012-13) 50%

Something for just about everyone option:
- $10 billion for thousands of programs like the AWM's travelling exhibitions scheme 25.0%
- $15 billion in tax reductions 37.5%
- $5 billion a year boost for safer and better roads and transport 12.5%
- $5 billion a year boost for schools 12.5%
- $5 billion a year boost for the environment 12.5%

Source of taxation data: Australian Bureau of Statistics, 'Taxation Revenue, Australia, 2012-13' (Catalogue 5506.0, released 28 May 2014)

References:

Drummond, M. L. (2002), 'Costing Constitutional Change: Estimating the Costs of Five Variations on Australia's Federal System', *Australian Journal of Public Administration*, Vol. 61, No. 4, December 2002.

Drummond, M. L. (2007), *Costing Constitutional Change: Estimates of the Financial Benefits of New States, Regional Governments, Unification and Related Reforms*, PhD thesis, University of Canberra.

Chapter 5

Local Sector Reform

Jim Snow

Removing a layer of government can reduce the total cost of government to taxpayers. Removing state governments also releases the potential for fortitude and enterprise in local communities, providing more scope and opportunities in their neighborhoods, businesses and administrations. In this chapter, I have drawn information gathered on a short experience as a local government community worker, and longer experiences as a parliamentarian, farmer and business owner and manager to argue that local governance based on uniform national laws can prepare communities to meet the challenges of a rapidly changing world.

Alternative models are outlined elsewhere in this book. All of them allow a national, legislating, sector and a locally or regionally based sector with more discretionary expenditure and with local by-laws. All assume a nation-wide public discussion on reform, backed by research.

Too many governments results in over-government. The federal, state and local governments are all involved in health, roads, social services, employment programs, land use, the environment and infrastructure among other matters. State government is one too many. More local decision-making should be unhindered by a 'middle man' in governance who soaks up funds, and reduces the efficiency of service delivery and infrastructure provision and prevents local adaptations to flexible laws.

Removal of the middle level allows large cities and non-metropolitan areas more control over their destinies and more freedom to set their populations and their economic goals. Some taxes, including payroll tax could be removed, reduced or rationalized. Dr Mark L. Drummond, a founding Convener of Beyond Federation completed a thesis, 'Costing

Constitutional Change', at the School of Business and Government at the University Canberra. He showed that unification and some regional models could bring financial benefits in the order of five to ten per cent, depending on the arrangements. In 2002 dollars the public sector benefit for the cost of government would have been $15 to $20 million in the public sector and $25 to $50 billion in the private sector. Drummond showed that under unitary government, including some proposed regional arrangements, there would be significant financial benefits from a uniform approach to health and education. Some local decision-making may be beneficial for other functions, notably transport and communications.

While he sees the retention of local councils as more immediately achievable, Drummond quoted a 1998 report by KPMG for the Property Council of Australia. It estimated that amalgamation of 177 NSW local councils into 20 would have saved $845 million or 22 per cent of the total local government expenditure of $3821 million. Twenty local governments in NSW would have been consistent with the Regional Organization of Councils approach.

Drummond also showed that extra costs near state borders 'appear to be especially significant in the area of health and community services, possibly in the order of $1 billion per annum'. Drummond's estimates of private business compliance costs to three sectors of government were substantiated by the work of Access Economics and the Business Regulation Review Unit .

Reform does not require changing the size of the Commonwealth House of Representatives or the Senate (if the Senate is retained, perhaps as a house representing regions). There is no intention to abolish states as a geographic entity in established and convenient arrangements; for example in sport.

Government of Metropolitan Regions

Reform can benefit the infrastructure and services in major metropolitan cities. One option would adopt some of the principles of the 'city state'. Singapore, a city state, spent 47 per cent of its expenditure on public transport and Perth four per cent, according to a 1998 report to the

World Bank[1]. With a whole of city approach population needs can be planned. Transport needs can be better coordinated and delivered more efficiently, thus avoiding problems such as traffic delays and tunnel disasters from high vehicles. The same applies to community services. Whole-of city administrations would benefit if its elected representatives were not expected to administer non-metropolitan areas and if its elected officials were better able to concentrate on city problems using the wealth of expertise on urban planning and strategies. (More than one planning and development division with localized public input structured into the system may suit some city populations and allow closer scrutiny).

The population drift to over-burdened cities could be expected to slow if other regional and more remote populations have more freedom to improve the viability of their local economies. In Britain following an economic decline in its northern districts, the geographer Eva G.R. Taylor estimated that 1000 more public servants in Leeds would lead to 7000 more jobs[2]. In Australia we have seen evidence of enterprising strategies that, with government support, have brought rewarding results, for example in tertiary education: Universities such as Southern Cross and New England have become major employers in regional Australia and have generated enormous economic advantage to their areas.

Government of Country Regions

However the decentralization of public and business offices and services to districts of lower socio-economic activity and incomes and to areas with potential resources and staffing has depended on the will and the incentive to retain them. Whole of state budgeting and the marginality of electorates for party candidates can override local need, local resilience and motivation as happened when several public service agencies were transferred from the northern rivers of NSW to other centres, including Sydney. A combination of appropriate distribution of government services and release from excessive oversight would allow localities to attract ideas and stimulate innovation: a better way to decentralize than by using economic incentives, hitherto usually found to be ineffective[3].

The ability to set by-laws under uniform legislation can free a reformed local government sector from inappropriate government control. All regions can benefit from this. Of the non-metropolitan cities and towns, few outside coastal areas can be rated as stable and very few as growth centres. There are over twenty stable or growing centres outside the present capitals. Of the inland cities Canberra, an industry (public service) city, is the largest. There is potential for growth in other cities and towns, particularly if their regional arrangements are strengthened and unhindered by superfluous state governments. In this way there is more scope for local initiatives that can lead to new opportunities for advancement, in remote primary industry and Aboriginal communities, as well as towns and cities.

The path for people, businesses and farmers to elected representatives would be clearer and shorter and more conducive to making better use of their inventive and innovative skills to develop marketing ideas to fruition. A wider array of jobs would keep more young people in their districts. Regions would be in a stronger position to coincide their skills and production with domestic and world demand. The cost of living for employees and the operating cost for employers would be reduced as would the large and growing cost of political representation by local industries and organizations to three levels of government, a cost eventually passed on to consumers.

Two main sectors should be involved in the receipt and expenditure of taxpayer and government enterprise funds, not three. The reasons are many. Garry Bowditch, the CEO of Wollongong University Smart Infrastructure facility has said that Australia's infrastructure development has been held back by 'the federal system', by inadequate attention by the Council of Australian Governments and by a lack of coordination with land use policies when developments, such as improved rail services, are considered[4]. Michael Deegan, the CEO of Infrastructure Australia, said that most submissions from state governments 'were not well thought out and were generally poorly explained.' There was a 'knowledge of, but unwillingness to address, widespread deficiencies' and he accused 'entrenched', 'truculent' bureaucracies of impeding progress with proposals without merit. 'Such willful attitudes test the patience of our elected masters, industry and the public'[5]

Regional Land-use Planning by Local Government

Corrupted planning and development processes have led to countless actions against state and local government representatives and public servants. Sacked councils have been a constant feature of governance following their corrupted planning processes. The removal of state governments would not remove the temptation but planning and development applications could be subject to approval by an elected regional body (under a regional option) or a regional planning body that includes local council representatives and trained public servants. This would reduce the probability of abuse. National legislators are more likely than state governments to set an effective line of appeal against decisions and are powerful enough to require ethical standards in the process. Regional planning authorities have already been established in New South Wales to deal with planning and development decisions. In Victoria the Westernport Regional Planning Authority was established by the state government in the early 1970s when it was obvious that huge regional industry, environmental and development challenges on the Mornington Peninsula and surrounds required a whole-of-region-approach[6]. Time has justified its appointment in spite of locals having to cope with three levels of government plus that regional authority.

A regional arrangement for planning and development allows a localized and feasible population policy. A previous Port Douglas council in Queensland was one of just a few local governments to adopt a population policy. A population policy developed through national and local resourcing could assist areas that have sought higher populations including Tasmania, South Australia and the Northern Territory as well as cities beset by the traffic and other problems associated with fast-growing populations.

Dysfunctional Governance

Citizens are disillusioned and confused by the federal system, especially the duplication of services, intergovernmental bickering, blaming and buck-passing. Confusion over which sector provides what services is very apparent in the offices of front line local, state and federal governments and those of their elected representatives.

State based statistics are equally confusing, yet these are frequently headlined in the media. The use of statistical state and territory comparisons of economic, employment, education, social well-being and health standards tells us little. Comparisons of regions are far more relevant. Tasmania illustrates the point; it receives bad media, and for no good reason is unfairly compared with other states as an economic failure. With the small capital, Hobart, and other cities such as Launceston and Burnie, a fairer comparison for Tasmania would be with non-metropolitan regions throughout Australia, many of them no more and very often less successful than the island's economy. An example at the time of writing is the 'food basket' surrounding Shepparton in Victoria, quoted as having eight per cent unemployment compared with Tasmania's 7.6 per cent, and that before a threat to close its food processing facility was implemented[7]. More remote areas have far higher unemployment and a thorough study of the successes and failures of our diverse regional economies including Tasmania, the Australian Capital Territory, the Northern Territory and some of the large, amalgamated local councils may be a useful prelude to reform.

The mainland state and territory boundaries are inappropriate. The old colonial boundaries ignore 'community of interest': The north of the Northern Territory and northern Western Australia have more in common than do Darwin and Alice Springs or Broome and Perth[8]. Northern Queensland has little in common with Brisbane and the Gold Coast and Tweed have more in common than either do with Sydney or Brisbane. Canberra is used for services and shopping far more than Sydney by Queanbeyan, Braidwood, Cooma, parts of the NSW south coast and Yass people[9]. However, inappropriate boundaries have harmed access to services, schools and even hospitals as well as the potential for economic and social development.

One reform option is to write a new constitution. Suggestions for consideration include a proposal for multi-member electorates elected by proportional representation, a move that would probably weaken the major political parties by increasing the number of locally oriented independent parliamentarians. Such parliaments have been less predictable, noisier and uncomfortable for its members and create uncertainty in a public unused to them, yet a close examination of the legislative records indicates a surprising efficiency and no lack of agreed legislation[10]. A national debate on constitutional reform would provide an opportunity for a wide-ranging public discussion on such proposals as well as other public issues, including a republic, constitutional recognition of a revitalized local sector and improved planning processes. Another option worth investigation and discussion includes giving the local or regional sector an agreed degree of voting power over national expenditure and revenue-raising, thus reducing prolonged and often costly negotiations.

There have been many moves for the establishment of new states as an attempt to improve local polity. New England in NSW, northern Queensland, the Gold Coast, the Tweed, Broken Hill and the Riverina are examples of populations seeking separation from their states. As far back as January 3, 1900 a public meeting in Kalgoorlie endorsed a petition to the Queen praying that the colony of WA might be divided into two[11].

Existing state powers would operate under most proposals for new states. This avoids a necessary look at which powers are appropriate for the national government and which are best placed in the local sector. New states with existing state powers are not recommended by Beyond Federation. Drummond looked at this issue: in 2002 dollars the extra cost of establishing new states with current state powers would be likely to be in the order of $1 billion per annum per new state, he said. If national systems were put in place in areas such as health and education the financial viability would be vastly improved[12].

Successful Regional Organizations

Finally, past criticisms of attempts at regionalism should not be ignored. Tony Sorensen, the Senior Lecturer in Geography and Planning at the University of New England described decentralization and regionalization policies as futile and he called for a move from the regionalism policies of state and federal governments. He said any 'high quality business and civic leadership appears to emerge accidently rather than through policy initiatives'[13]. Many attempts at imposed regionalism have faded away. However some cooperative efforts have continued (regional planning and health authorities, WESROC (the Western Regional Organization of councils), Illawarra cooperating councils, recycling cooperation between Canberra, Yass and the Monaro and Albury-Wodonga are examples). Unless state or national governments perceive a vested interest in support for amalgamation or regionalization, it does not happen and when it does it can be abandoned with a change in government[14]. Many of the unpromising attempts may have vitalized civic life if they had not lacked political arrangements that 'reflect the identity of the participants'[15].

The federal system has inhibited actions directed at improving democracy and reducing the cost of government. Australia deserves uniform legislation when appropriate and a local sector with the financial backing and appropriate options to do its work. Outcomes will improve for the environment, transport, infrastructure, social services and many other policy areas. The federal system has made local government the permanently dependent child of the states while abandoning it to a circle of declining reputation, dismissal in some areas and, too frequently, corruption, The local sector needs to be able to innovate and use its expertise and experience to responsibly encourage more economic and social development. A hidebound Constitution has failed to evolve with the times and has delivered a superfluous, interfering, inadequate, bickering and costly state sector transposed from the old British colonies, a sector that has inhibited good governance.

Endnotes

1   Study for the World Bank *Moving the Economy* by Stephen Laube, Mur-

doch University, report in West Australian newspaper (11 July 1998) of a conference in Toronto, Canada.

2   Eva G.R. Taylor, English geographer, historian and writer.

3   Successful exceptions include Akubra Hats, based in Kempsey and decentralization subsidies to benefit Maryborough in Victoria. St Arnaud in Victoria had a brassiere factory subsidized which employed many women for some years until a change of state government in the 1950s removed its subsidy.

4   Garry Bowditch interviewed by Nick Reinberger of ABC Illawarra radio morning show on 28 January 2014.

5   Michael Deegan quoted by the Sydney Morning Herald on February 8, 2014.

6   The establishment of the Westernport Regional Planning Authority by the Victorian government in the early 1970s was associated with new steelworks at Hastings in Victoria and increasing demands on local governments on and around the Mornington Peninsula. The writer was in business at Hastings and operated a stud farm at Red Hill on the Peninsula at the time.

7   Figures quoted by the Liberal Member for Murray, Dr Sharman Stone, 7.30 Report, February 4, 2014.

8   This view was expressed to me when I interviewed Broome and Karatha residents for a magazine article.

9   I found this when I was Secretary of the South Eastern Regional Council for Social Development between 1975 and 1977. The council members included local governments from the Monaro, Snowy Mountains, South East Coast and Southern Tablelands, community representatives from those areas and the ACT and the ACT Council of Social Services,

10   The long-standing, though often uneasy and suppressed relationship between the Liberal and National parties is one example and the recent, equally uneasy but more publicized experiences of the Rudd and Gillard governments (2007 to 2013) is another.

11   Manning Clark *A History of Australia* Vol 5 p 174.

12   See Drummond 2007 p ii.

13   Tony Sorenson, writing in *Agenda* , 'a journal of policy analysis and reform', vol 1 1994 pp33-44

14   Regional health boards lasted for some years in NSW and the Westernport Regional Planning Authority persisted in Victoria.

15   Michael J. Sandel, *Democracy's Discontent* (Beknap Press, Harvard University ISBN 0-674-19745-3

Chapter 6

Shed a Tier

Max Bradley

Australia is a large diverse country, with a small area that follows the costal fringe in the southeast area where there is fertile farming land with a rainfall that is sufficient to make this area profitable for small farms. A large area of the continent is dry and arid, making farming into to a big area operation. This led to cities, towns and communities growing where there were numbers of people sufficient to support such places. This has lead to having three cities and their close regions having half the entire population of this nation and many areas with small towns many kilometers apart and large areas with few people. All these people have a right to a fair and equitable system of government. To have a system of government that can be effective to all the citizens and their needs is a huge problem and one that the Shed a Tier model will overcome.

The Shed a Tier Model

The system of governance and government described here is a simple straightforward system that will meet the needs of the citizens and communities of this nation for the next century. It will be controlled by the people, for the people and be close to the people. This system will be able to achieve local outcomes at a local and community level, and national outcomes at a national level, and will be fair, equitable, and democratic. This system will be better able to defend Australians and Australia and work with the rest of the world to make the world a better place. The citizens will have control over the whole process of government, in the way the government is elected, and during the government's term in office. The design of this system can be the benchmark for the rest of the world. This system is put together using some of the existing parts of the present system, and will streamline the whole structure of government

Issues with the present system

Listed below are some of the many major problems with the present system of government and many exist because of the six state governments and two territory governments and a federal government.

1. There are seventeen houses of parliament.

2. There are 754 politicians.

3. The huge cost of having more than one parliament.

4. The huge cost of having more that one government.

5. The huge cost of having such a disjointed system of government.

6. Different laws and rules

7. Different education systems.

8. Disjointed health and aged care systems.

9. Different police forces.

10. Complicated system of government.

11. Far too many politicians.

12. Far too many bureaucrats.

13. Buck passing between governments.

14. Communities have little control over local issues.

15. Lack of interest in politics by the people.

16. Too many people making laws and rules.

17. The whole system of government is geared to money.

18. People have no control over politicians after they are elected.

19. The system has taken away the need for voters to put any thought into what they vote for.

20. The voting system has many flaws.

21. Inadequate safeguards against corrupt politicians and governments.

22. The inability of government to pass legislation because of the two-house system.

Many of these problems have huge cost implications for the people and the economy of the country. This money can be redirected and better spent on the people of Australia, for the benefit of all Australians. The Shed a Tier model that is presented here will solve many of these problems, and being simple and understandable it is hoped that more people will take an interest in the national government and its workings, as well as take an active part in their community and local council. One aim of this model is to achieve the greatest effect, with the least amount of change and disruption to our everyday lives. By using part of the present federal government and the local council areas from the present system an easy understanding of the changes and their effects can be seen.

The major change will be the abolition of the six state and two territory governments, with their powers, responsibilities, assets, territory and rights going to a national government. Any of the assets of the abolished governments that can be used by the local council and the community, will be shifted into community ownership. The new Australian government will take over the old federal government and will continue with the responsibilities it had plus the powers, responsibilities, assets, territory and rights that have been granted by the people from the abolished governments. This will then become a true Australian government for the whole of Australia and its people. The present states can still exist as areas.

The new Australian government will be elected by using the present federal electorates and will use the federal parliament house in Canberra. Local councillors will be elected as they are now, and will continue with present roles in their present council areas.

Every community, town, village, area, district, or region will have ownership and control of the infrastructure that it needs and has use of. A hospital will be owned by the community in the area that it serves. The local hall will be owned by the community that uses it. Local roads will be owned by the local shire or council and the people who use them, and they will be responsible for the upkeep. Community committees or council will be the trustees. There will be no restriction on the private ownership of such infrastructure. The major infrastructure that is used by the majority of the people and beyond the capability of the local council and community, such as highways, major roads, dams, power stations, airports etc, will be funded and controlled by the new Australian government.

The new Australian government will be responsible for the funding and for the setting of policy on all health issues and aged care. The implementation of this policy will be by area health boards, such as in NSW. At a local community level this will be by a local committee, who will come from the community and from local council. There will be an Australian health board whose members will be nominated by the people who are involved in health and aged care and their role will be to assist the minister for health and aged care, plan what resources are needed and where resources should be placed. Funding for health will be on a need and per capita basis.

The new Australian government will set up the Australian Police Force that will take all the present police systems and form one force. This Australian Police Force will have a permanent presence in as many communities on a needs basis, as practicably as possible. The large cities will each have one police district and have police stations spread across them, to give as many 24-hour stations as possible. In regional and rural areas many of the present police districts can be used. In rural towns the police, ambulance, fire services, etc., will be set up in one command centre so as there will be someone on duty at all times to man radios etc.

The new Australian Government will fund and set policy and overall curriculum for Education. Funding will go to schools on a per pupil basis, with a system of allowances for remoteness or other disadvantages. At a local school level the funding will be controlled by a school board. These school boards will be selected by the community involved in the school.

The Murray Darling Basin will have a board consisting of members of the Australian government whose electorates are in this region and the same number of local councillors whose councils are in the area. The funding to achieve outcomes will come from the Australian government on a needs basis. The same system will apply to other regions e.g. Great Barrier Reef.

Your local council or shire will have little change to what it does now. There will be the added role and responsibility of forming the committees that will be set up for schools, health, police etc. The role of the local council will be to have these committees formed and to make sure the members understand and carry out their role. Local councillors will form these committees if there is no support from the community and these committees will work under Australian government guidelines. It will be the local council manager's responsibility to inform these committees of their legal responsibility and to report to the appropriate minister.

The major cities such as Melbourne and Sydney will have a regional administration board, which will again consist of members of the Australian parliament whose electorates are within the greater metropolitan region and the same number of councillors from the local councils within the region. The role of these boards will be to oversee and coordinate infrastructure within the city region. These boards will meet when needed.

For the present local government to make the transition to the Shed a Tier model, all the councils would continue, as they exist within their present local government act. Over a two-year time frame all councils will shift to the Australian Local Council Act, which will be derived from all the better parts of all the state Local Council Act. The Australian local council act will be reviewed every four years, and updated so as to achieve the best outcomes for the people and their communities.

The Shed a Tier model described here is simple and an easy change as it only replaces who is in charge of some parts of the present system. Powers are taken from state ministers' control and placed under the Australian government. This part of the Shed a Tier model can be put in place without Constitutional change. Section 111 of the Constitution allows for this to happen. "The Parliament of a state may surrender any part of a state to the commonwealth; and upon acceptance thereof by the commonwealth, such part of the state shall become subject to the exclusive jurisdiction of the Commonwealth".

The benefits of the Shed a Tier model will be huge but the changes to everyday life will be little.

Chapter 7

The Kemsley Oration Melbourne, 2013

Elizabeth Proust

Thank you for the invitation to deliver the Kemsley Oration today. This Oration is held annually to honour Sir Alfred Kemsley whose long career made a very significant contribution to town planning in Victoria. I am conscious of the contribution also of the very distinguished people who have delivered this Oration before me. They have been politicians, journalists, public servants, architects; all of whom had a deep knowledge of matters such as planning for cities, and/or a deep love of this particular city, or of cities in general. Some of the people making past Orations have been colleagues of mine, and many have made a major contribution, both through this Oration and elsewhere, to the thinking about a range of issues related to city life and planning.

They are also a very eclectic group of people. I imagine that my own career might be seen to be similarly eclectic. My main involvement in the matters about which I will speak was when I was Chief Executive of the City of Melbourne between 1990 and 1995, and to a more limited extent for 3 years after that when I was Secretary of the Department of Premier and Cabinet. I remain an interested observer in many matters relevant here, but have had no direct involvement, let alone influence, since 1998.

So, what follows is very much a personal perspective on matters relating to our cities, but principally Melbourne. I have drawn upon recent State Government reports, those of the Grattan Institute, and of the Committee for Melbourne in putting together this Oration. But, of course, the views expressed, are my own.

I want to cover a number of topics, none of them in depth, but I want to stimulate some thinking and discussion about the issues which our cities face over the next decades as they expand and change.

Primarily we need a vision for our cities, which is beyond electoral cycles and short term planning horizons; and we need to engage people so that they understand and feel that they are part of planning and designing our future. We have had no shortage of plans over the decades; many of them have contained the word "vision" but most of them have lacked a true vision. By this I mean that many of them have lacked imagination, creativity, innovation and the power to inspire. In most cases, they were written by a committee and this is always evident.

Before I elaborate further on this, let me give you an example of how I believe that we make almost everything we do in this country over complicated and slow. If we were acting in this way to ensure that there was proper consultation, there would be less cause for complaint. But it is not consultation that slows us down; it is our federation and the sheer number and layers of organizations that involve themselves in decision making. More is not always better!

Let me give you an example. In April last year, I read a story which caused me to shudder. The then Federal Government put out a press release "Gillard Government supports city growth areas". Now, that may look like a statement that is not contentious and might have passed almost unnoticed. But, in the text of the release it read "That's why Federal Labor has ended the Commonwealth's self-imposed, decade long exile from our major cities and is again engaging with the states and territories and local councils to bring about a much needed urban renaissance".

My response to that statement, then and now is "Let's keep federal bureaucrats and politicians out of our cities"! Urban renewal, or renaissance, will not come about from a plethora of Canberra committees, however well intentioned, nor from a slew of studies directed by Canberra. Australia does not have four cities in the world's top 10 most livable cities (with Melbourne leading the pack) by accident, or because Canberra has been in exile from our cities. In Melbourne, we have achieved this distinction because of an elusive combination of people's pride in the city, good planning over almost 180 years, and good economic policies which combine to make Melbourne a vibrant, lively place where people and businesses want to live, work and invest.

If we were planning our federation today, we would not feel the tyranny of distance in this country as our forebears did; and technology has enabled much that was unimaginable when the current system was being planned. We would hopefully devise a system with only two levels of government – a national one, and regional one, based on units smaller than today's states, but much larger than our local government areas.

This change, of course, will not happen, so we have to make our federation work. For me this means, getting the Commonwealth out of service delivery (its track record is poor), significantly reducing the size of the Commonwealth bureaucracy where it purports to deal with key delivery areas (health, education, etc) and certainly keeping them out of matters in which they have little expertise and no right to meddle.

But, clearly we need Canberra's money – this, of course is the issue that goes to the heart of our federation's problems and challenges. The Commonwealth has the money, and the states have the obligations to provide costly services without access to growth taxes such as income tax and GST.

Infrastructure is a key factor in this equation. The majority of Australians live in our capital cities and this trend will continue. The commute to work in each of those cities is getting longer, jobs are largely located in the CBDs, or within relative proximity to those CBDs, where housing costs are high. Young people and those on lower incomes are forced to the outskirts of our cities, where public transport is rare and car reliance increases.

Governments increasingly claim not to be able to fund the infrastructure needed to deal with the problems facing our cities. Yet all of us know that failure to deal with these problems is only exacerbating them. We need to find collaborative ways to fund our infrastructure projects. Increasingly the debate about which infrastructure, and how to pay for it, has become polarized. It is a fruitless debate about "public transport OR roads". We need to find the "AND" word here: public transport AND roads. If you are in the inner suburbs, you will find no shortage of posters proclaiming "public transport not toll roads". Whether we like it or not, we are a car dependent city, and must find better ways to integrate both public and private transport.

If we do not find ways to engage the community in the debate, including engaging to find appropriate compromises, the problems caused by decades of neglect of our infrastructure will only be compounded.

I will use just one example here: the large number of railway level crossings at grade in Melbourne. There are over 170 such crossings which add to traffic congestion, probably also to road rage, increase pollution, and lower productivity. The Committee for Melbourne is doing some good work here in proposing ways in which these crossings can be removed, including by proposing some alternative funding mechanisms. Each removal is said to cost about $100 million so clearly there is no quick fix. Again, if we were planning Melbourne from scratch, we would never have allowed these crossings to exist in the first place.

I have already referred to the trend which sees people on lower incomes forced to the fringes of our cities. How do we ensure that we do not have a city that is fractured by lack of social cohesion? One of the key differentiators between a livable city, and those which are certainly not livable is in the more difficult to define, but still tangible factors, such as a sense of belonging, identity and relationships. The work that the Committee for Melbourne and Mission Australia is doing in this area is vital. As our city grows, how do we ensure that it belongs to all of us, and not just to the wealthy and well connected? Transport and other services such as good quality health care and education are a key part of this mix and must be planned for and provided equitably.

Governments are often called upon to create jobs in outer suburban areas to deal with some of these problems. They do this by offering incentives, usually tax incentives, to businesses to relocate, or to build new centres of employment in these suburbs. The Grattan Institute has found that there is little evidence that these policies work.

I want to use an example to illustrate this point. Despite changing technology many people, firms and clients want to work in close proximity with similar firms. I am a director of the global engineering firm, Sinclair Knight Merz (SKM). Our Melbourne office until a few years ago was located in Armadale, with good access to public transport, close to major roads, and with plenty of off street parking. When the lease was coming up for renewal, SKM made the decision to move over 800 people in Armadale into Flinders Street in the city. Here accommodation is more expensive, and off street parking difficult or costly. The reasons for the move to the CBD by SKM included having access to a deeper pool of employees, including potential graduates, being more accessible to clients, and staff having more ability to network with clients, with government and with other professional organizations.

Let me now turn to an issue, which I know can be polarizing. I have said that we would not create 3 levels of government if we were starting now. However, we can take steps that would rationalize our governments, and make them more effective and efficient. I have already referred to the need to reduce the encroachment of the federal bureaucracy. Not only is 3 layers, one too many; we also have too many units of local government which are too small to be effective or efficient.

The local government changes brought about by the Kennett Government were sensible changes but in hindsight did not go far enough. The pre 1993 boundaries were essentially 19th century ones, certainly in Melbourne and our regional cities. The 1993 changes brought the boundaries up to about the 1920's or 1930's. While the number of local councils in Victoria was reduced from about 210 to 79 today, that number is still too large; as is the number of 30 or so councils which cover Melbourne.

Brisbane should be a model for us. It is of sufficient size and scale to be able to plan for all its services effectively and efficiently, yet, via the ward system, still able to ensure that local needs are met. It serves the people of

Brisbane well and should be considered for Melbourne. Of course, I have no illusions about the nature of the forces that would be ranged against such an idea but we should have the debate. Melbourne is now of a size and scale that demands city-wide planning, vision and governance. Are we up for this debate?

Now, some would argue that the new Metropolitan Planning Authority (MPA) can take on much of this role. It will be charged with implementing "Plan Melbourne" and with ensuring that Melbourne is open to business investment. The MPA may well be able to coordinate planning and streamline decisions but it is not an elected body and of course cannot do all that a body such as the City of Brisbane does.

The mention of size and scale brings me to population. This is another topic on which it seems difficult to have an "adult" conversation. What might Melbourne's population be in 2050? Should we be scared of that?

You will have seen the recent ABS projections which predict that almost 10 million migrants arriving in Australia will increase our population to more than 40 million by 2060, and to more than 50 million by 2100. That is still a small population by global standards, certainly given our land mass and resources (probably excluding water). Most of this population increase will be in the capital cities, not regional or rural areas.

By 2060, Melbourne will have 8.5 million people, double our population today. By 2050, Melbourne is predicted by the ABS to have 1.2 million more people than the State Government assumed in its "Plan Melbourne" released last month. We are already, by world standards, a large (in geographic terms) city but our growth cannot continue to be at the expense of valuable farmland and mountain areas. We must find a way to deal with the density of our city.

Let me turn to "Plan Melbourne" as it represents the State Government's most recent statement on key issues for Melbourne, a number of which I have already covered. The document is one that aims to be the planning strategy document for Melbourne to 2050. Its vision is stated to be "Melbourne will be a global city of opportunity and choice" achieved by:

- Protecting the suburbs

- Developing in defined areas near services and infrastructure

- Creating a clearer and simpler planning system with improved decision making

- Rebalancing growth between Melbourne and regional Victoria, and

- Identifying an investment and infrastructure pipeline

    "Plan Melbourne" rightly points out Melbourne's advantages, including the vibrancy of the city, its educated and multicultural workforce, our university sector, and our sporting and arts heritage. On reading the document it strikes you that the consultation process threw up a number of challenges for the success or otherwise of the implementation of "Plan Melbourne"; challenges which have led to the demise of similar planning documents in the past.

The themes that emerged from this consultation process included:

- People would like to see the unique character of their neighbourhoods preserved (code for NIMBY?)

- Public transport is a clear priority (who pays?)

- People support increased density in defined locations (again, code for NIMBY?)

- Employment opportunities should be decentralized to create more local jobs in different parts of Melbourne (see Grattan Institute report)

- Melbourne in 2050 will be inclusive and accepting of change (but not now?)

Clearly I cannot cover all of "Plan Melbourne" here, and many of you will know and understand its ramifications better than I do. But I was struck, but not surprised, by a number of responses to the document. The

Labor Member for Wills, Kelvin Thomson, claimed that immigration and therefore population growth were the real problems (presumably solved by putting up a sign "Melbourne is full"!) just as former Premier, Bob Carr, attempted to do in Sydney, with a notably detrimental impact on Sydney's growth (or lack thereof) for over a decade.

Michael Buxton, Professor of Environment and Planning at RMIT, writing in the Age, blamed the capture of government by business interests for the likely failure of the plan. And Robert Nelson, a lecturer at Monash University, also writing in the Age, said we, the public, the people of Melbourne are to blame for the problem. He said "The problem is not the minister. The problem is the public. Planning in Australia has been impossible for decades, not because we've had to submit to the indignity of foreign capital but because our urbanism is kneecapped by a complacent backyard isolationism that keeps us in cars and keeps us sprawling beyond our fringes". (I had forgotten the emotions and the language that a good planning stoush could generate!)

Let me draw these strands to a conclusion. I assume that most of you in the audience tonight are professional planners with a deep knowledge and commitment to planning, to using your skills and experience to help ensure that we provide the very best options for our cities and communities; that we learn from past mistakes and that we ensure that the cities we leave to future generations are even better than the ones we inherited. Whether you are a planner, or whether like me, an interested observer and participant in the life of cities, and in this one in particular, we all have a role in ensuring that the debate and decision making processes around our city's future are well informed by economic realities, based on long term goals and the need to take people on that journey to the future.

Chapter 8

Governing without State Governments

Anthony Nicholas

Summary

The role of state governments could be superseded by the Commonwealth and local governments using the functional regional administrations already in existence and creating similar entities where required. A new tier of government would not be required, although some minor reorganization of existing national and local governments would be necessary.

The Role of State Governments

The role of state governments extends in three directions. First, they control local governments, second, they have created numerous specialized agencies to carry out specific tasks and third, they create legislation within their state jurisdictions that often has nation-wide effects.

State governments manage a plethora of authorities, agencies, etc., some of which could be administered by local governments, such as public libraries and water supply. Others are of national significance, for example, inquiries into sexual abuse that is now a proper task of the national government. Many programs, found in several states could be nationally integrated to achieve more efficient and effective government. The third role of framing legislation of nation-wide significance is clearly a proper role for the Commonwealth, because the effects are spread beyond state borders.

Typically, the departments of government divide their responsibilities into functions and subdivide their functions into regional administrations. Subject to the over-riding policies of the government, functional regional administrations provide government services to their host communities. They are the 'coal-face'.

Without state governments the most efficient and effective option for their replacement must be sought and this would require using just so many of the existing tiers of government that would be necessary and sufficient for the role, rather than creating new 'regional governments'. Within the various functions of government there is a hierarchy of tasks to be undertaken; the Commonwealth should take over all those tasks that require national regulation or coordination and local governments, in addition to their traditional roles and acting in collaboration, would undertake the remaining regional tasks of creating and supervising the operation of functional regional administrations.

Functional Regions

The Commonwealth and state governments have already created regional administrations to manage many of their functions, each function having a characteristic regional structure. These functional regions have three essential qualities: first, their geography is characterized by their particular function, resulting in different regional boundaries for each function. Second, their shape and size may vary over time, according to the scope of service, changes in population, improved infrastructure and advances in technology. Third, their size is designed to maintain, within each region, adequate expertise in their particular functions.

As outlined above, there will be a natural disparity between the coverage of the various functional regions. The functional regional structures for fire-fighting or waste re-cycling do not match each other, nor does either match the functional regions for schools or community health. Differences can be illustrated by observing the disparity in the numbers and sizes of regions created for the different functions of government. By contrast, the imposition of fixed territorial boundaries on different functions would lead to widespread inefficiency, worse than the states, because there would be so many more borders.

Table 1 shows a sample of functional regions that have been created to match the requirements of several government functions in NSW and Victoria. The disparity between the numbers of regions indicates significant mismatching among the various functional regions.

The nature of functional regions is illustrated in maps of the of the Departments of Health in the various states, available via the hyperlinks:

yourHealth - Local Hospital Networks and Our Regions - Department of Health, Victoria, Australia.

NSW Local Land Service regions can be seen at http://www.lls.nsw.gov. au/ and Victorian Catchment Management regions are shown at http://www.depi.vic.gov.au/about-us/our-regions.

Each functional region could be monitored by an adequately resourced board drawn from the pool of constituents, perhaps with representation from the Commonwealth, giving local communities a measure of responsibility for priorities in the allocation of resources

Table 1   Numbers of Some Functional Regions

Function	Regions	Comment
NEW SOUTH WALES		
Bureau of Meteorology	16	
Ministry of Health	15	Plus Albury/Wodonga Health
NSW Public School Regions	10	
Regional Organizations of Councils	18	
Police Local Area Commands	80	
Police Regions	5	
Catchment Management	13	Some regions could merge across state borders.
Water Supply Utilities - Country NSW	105	
Local Land Services Regions	11	Includes agricultural services
Commonwealth Aged Care	16	
Medicare Locals	17	Commonwealth government agencies

VICTORIA		
Country Fire Authority regions	24	
Total fire Ban Districts	5	
Waste Management Groups	13	Includes recycling
Department of Health regions	8	
Library Service regions	14	Run by Local governments
Water Supply Authorities	19	
Catchment Management Authorities	11	
Commonwealth Aged Care	9	Based on Statistical Local Areas
Medicare Locals	17	Includes districts north of the Murray

An example of a working functional regional administration is the Hume Region of the Victorian Health Department, arguably the most effective of the state health departments. This functional region is run by a team of dedicated and experienced public servants based in Wangaratta. It covers twelve local government areas plus Albury-Wodonga Health, in northeast Victoria. It includes four primary care partnerships, contains twenty-two public hospitals and six private hospitals The population is about two hundred and seventy-thousand, with low rankings for most health conditions, for socio-economic statistics and for the availability of public transport. The funding for the regional operations, in common with other Victorian Department of Health regions, is set by complex formulae initiated in the late 1980s, and introduced in 1993 after thorough testing. These procedures and formulae are continually refined and could be adapted to achieve results in the health services of other states. The two major hospitals are supervised by boards of directors selected by the state government from applicants drawn from the communities served by those hospitals. These directors, and those of other government and community facilities, are guided by a monumental program of governance education organized by the Victorian state government. Would the current [2014] Commonwealth government's faith in 'competitive federalism' require the other eight governments in Australia to replicate this program, or could it be more cost-effective to have just one for the nation. In 2011, the Commonwealth began establishing Medicare Locals, over a brace of sixty-one localities related to the recognized need for information on primary health care. The agency is based in Canberra and locality boundaries extend across the Murray on the NSW/VIC border, while other state borders are fully respected. These agencies perform a valuable role in primary health care by connecting community health needs with available services. Within the Hume health department region the locality boundaries are compatible with the existing state government regions but appear to be different from the states' districts elsewhere.

Without state governments, functional administrative regions would be unchanged, except for amalgamation of regions adjoining state borders. The people that run the day-to-day operations of government departments or ministries would continue in their usual roles and the clients of these agencies would find their usual relationships intact. The major change would be that the national tasks of management of these regional administrations would be the responsibility of the Commonwealth, and regional and local tasks would be the responsibility of one or more boards of management for each region; these boards could be made up of nominees of the constituent local governments and other stakeholders. Some state governments have not yet established functional regional administrations for all or even many of the tasks of government being run from head quarters in the capital cities. Without state governments, it is clear that adequate time would be needed to create functioning regional administrations and develop their management structures; such a program would require a transitory provision in a re-written constitution that would automatically lapse when those conditions were satisfied.

As a hypothetical example of a functional region for the task of school education, it would be feasible for a regional school program to make allowance for economic distress, or climate [by varying school attendance times], or the ethnic make-up of a community within the scope of the national function. Adaptions would be made to cater for conditions such as sparse population or urban congestion. Perhaps surfing could become a topic within the science curriculum in some regions, as has out-back wildlife in one appropriate region. The national education function should remain national, while encouraging regional and local variants to flourish.

Anthony Nicholas

Territorial Regions

Some commentators, advocating the replacement of state governments, take a 'top-down' approach and grandly suggest that new regional governments should replace them. In some suggested reforms, these territories are also electoral districts of the national parliament, supposedly enhancing the nation's democratic credentials.

The implication behind those suggestions is that each regional government would be responsible for providing services to the territory within its fixed boundaries. These territories would be better described as 'mini-states' than regions, because their borders are prescribed from a superior authority, rather than from the needs of the constituent communities. According to most dictionaries, a region *'is an area of the earth's surface with a defining characteristic'.* The several documented proposals that actually delineate 'territorial regions' in the form of maps or specifications, show territories that would be too small for some functions, too large for others and inappropriate for most. In general, they do not fit the definition of 'region'. For example, one proposal suggests that some local government areas would extend across the entire E-W width of Queensland, about 1450km; this is stretching the idea of 'local' a bit too far.

Functions such as water supply or catchment management are unlikely to fit easily into territorial boundaries drawn from criteria based on presumed community interests and vice versa. Indeed, the introduction of regional governments, would impose a jig-saw puzzle of boundaries across existing functional regions, leaving the legs of a typical function detached from its body in another territory. They would re-create the problems that arise at state borders under existing state jurisdictions, but many times worse, because there are many more proposed territorial regions, than states; about sixty instead of six. The reorganization of service agencies, ministries and departments to conform to territorial regions would be time-consuming, expensive and operationally sub-optimal.

Grass Roots

Australia has a population of more than 24 million who collectively belong to six hundred thousand not-for-profit organizations. These organizations range from small local clubs to international agencies, a fact which suggests that communities are capable of organizing themselves to achieve agreed outcomes, with minimal help from government or politicians.

There are also some 564 local governments, varying in size from several hundred people to over a million, some of which have been in operation since the 1860s. For the most part, local governments operate effectively with little constructive intervention from the state governments to which they are responsible. Many collaborate with neighbouring local governments in *Regional Organizations of Councils* to further their mutual interests. If local governments were required to take on an expanded role, there is little doubt that the new challenge could be met adequately, because, as past experience indicates, new challenges attract more talent from local communities.

Functional regions must be adjusted from time to time and some new ones may be required. The most appropriate instrumentalities to undertake those tasks would be the local governments involved or the functional agency itself. Least appropriate would be the central government; its record of top-down delineation of regions is not reassuring. Another set of ideas for new regions are top-down proposals for reforming the federation by creating new 'regions'. It is worth noting again the common usage of the term 'region': *an area of the earth's surface with a defining characteristic.* Drawing a shape on a map with a felt-tipped pen does not provide a defining characteristic, particularly in light of the popularity of felt-tip pens. One recent example of this practice is Richard Murray's proposed new constitution, which is also discussed Chapter 1 and in Appendix 1 near the end of this book. 'Regions' offered there are mainly geometric sub-divisions of the original states and are properly described as 'ministates', not regions.

Conclusion

Without state governments there is already an adequate governmental structure in place and that could be further developed to efficiently and effectively carry out the various roles of state governments. Functional regional administrations are an important, but largely invisible element of this structure, through which many government services are delivered to their host communities. They are the 'coal-face' of government.

Chapter 9

The Formation of the Australian Federal Constitution

Reflections on a Conference about Andrew Inglis Clark

Klaas Woldring

Why was the federal unification structure adopted for Australia in the first place? Was it seen as a flexible, democratic arrangement that could be adjusted easily to accommodate changing circumstances? Who were the principal architects? In this chapter we reflect on the historical role of Andrew Inglis Clark, a Tasmanian engineer and lawyer, who was much impressed with the American federation and American culture independent of the British Empire. On 8 November 2013, four members of *Beyond Federation* attended a free Conference in Parliament House, Canberra, organized by the Senate and called, 'The Truest Patriotism': Andrew Inglis Clark and the Building of an Australian Nation.

An impressive array of speakers was assembled; contributors Professor Helen Irving (Sydney) and The Hon. Robert French AC, Chief Justice of the High Court were apologies but their papers are available at the conference web site. The views of some of these are briefly referred to in this chapter. Some source material by the Senate, ANU and University of Tasmania Library was also provided. Others' relevant views are referred to as well. It would be fair to say that the Conference stimulated us to put a book together on the more radical views on governance and federalism in our own time.

In that context, a discussion of Clark as an innovator and framer of a new political system fits this volume. Although almost forgotten by some,

Clark's initiatives and impact during the 1890s Conventions can hardly be disputed. Clark (1848 – 1907) who, first qualified as an engineer and worked for some time in his Father's business in Hobart, continued with studies in law at age 24. He was admitted to practice in 1878. In 1874 he started a journal, 'Quadrilateral', which apart from poetry also carried articles about federalism, proportional representation and responsible government. This publication was followed by a discussion group, the Minerva Club. Politically ambitious, he became a member of the Tasmanian House of Assembly (for 15 years) and was Attorney General (for 8 years). In 1876 the American Club celebrated the 1776 Declaration of American Independence. He travelled twice to the US and had influential friends there. Clark was a Tasmanian delegate to the Australian Federation Conference in 1890, and the National Australasian Convention in 1891 for which he prepared a draft of a federal constitution. He achieved great distinction as a judge and legal thinker and published 'Studies in Australian Constitution Law (1901/1905),' still highly regarded in academe. He was involved in establishing the University of Tasmania.

Prior to entering Parliament, Clark was regarded with some suspicion on account of his radical nationalism and being an 'ultra-republican'. He was attacked in the Hobart Mercury and in the Launceston Examiner. Some saw him as a revolutionary and a communist. In fact, he was an admirer of Abraham Lincoln, a true democrat who wanted government not to benefit any particular class. He also admired Mazzini and the Risorgimento movement.

The Conference

Most of the Conference speakers, all well versed in Clark's background and ideas, see him as the primary or principal architect of Australia's federal Constitution. Irving questions that, somewhat tongue-in-cheek, by referring to that label as perhaps 'overrated'.

Professor John Williams, discussing Clark's draft Constitution prior to the 1891 conference, writes:

"At the Melbourne 1890 national conference, called to discuss whether the time was indeed 'ripe' to advance the federation of the colonies, Inglis Clark played a significant role in directing the discussion as to the type of federal model. Unlike many delegates Inglis Clark was willing to engage in detailed discussion as to the merits of the Canadian and American federal systems. He quickly nailed his colours to the American alternative. As he told delegates:

The question of the Canadian Constitution has been several times mentioned in the course of our proceedings, and its difference from that of the United States has been somewhat touched upon. For my part I would prefer the lines of the American Union to those of the Dominion of Canada. In fact, I regard the Dominion of Canada as an instance of amalgamation rather than of federation, and I am convinced that the different Australian Colonies do not want absolute amalgamation. What they want is federation in the true sense of the word.

The decision to hold a second Constitutional Convention in Sydney in 1891 prompted Inglis Clark to make his major contribution to the process of drafting the Constitution. He arrived again prepared to advance the American approach to federalism and the judicature. Prior to the Convention he had circulated a draft constitution bill and memorandum to the Tasmanian delegates, as well as to Sir Henry Parkes, George Higginbotham, Edmund Barton and perhaps others he knew for their consideration. In Inglis Clark the federal movement not only had a scholar of constitutional law but also an individual deeply committed to the creation of the nation".

The 1891 Draft Constitution

Williams continues:

"The influence Inglis Clark has had on the drafting of the Australian Constitution is multifaceted. It covers both the content and the structure of the current Constitution as well as its interpretation. Beyond this it is interesting to review the constitutional phrases or areas on regulation that he added or omitted when drafting his Constitution.

Inglis Clark's draft Constitution Bill has been the subject of much academic consideration and its influence over the ultimate structure of the Australian Constitution has been confirmed. As F.M. Neasey has demonstrated only eight of Inglis Clark's ninety-six clauses failed to find their way into the final Australian Constitution, a testimony to his influence on the process.

There are many counterfactual questions to be asked with respect to Inglis Clark's draft Constitution. Perhaps the most intriguing would be the amending provision. Geoffrey Sawer has famously described Australia as constitutionally speaking to be a 'frozen continent'. The record of unsuccessful constitutional amendment has informed this description. The amending provision suggested by Inglis Clark was in clause 93. It required that:

'This Act may at any time be amended by the Federal Parliament, but no amendment made by the Federal Parliament shall have any force or effect until it has been confirmed by the Parliaments of not less than two-thirds of the Provinces included in the Federal Dominion of Australasia at the time such Amendment is made.'

Undoubtedly this formula for constitutional amendment lacks the democratic authority of section 128, which requires the electors to endorse any proposed change. However, it is arguable that many technical amendments to the Constitution may have fared better under Inglis Clark's amending provision. However, other more fundamental changes—such as becoming a republic—would obviously require the direct involvement of the people to have legitimacy."

During the discussion of the comprehensive Williams' paper, Professor Henry Reynolds commented on the amendment issue:

"There is a fundamental point, John, that when the Constitution was framed, there were not political parties in the sense that we know them today. As we know, if you have got a referendum and the political parties take different sides, as they almost certainly do for political reasons, even though they might have supported the thing in the past, the opposition will oppose it because the government is proposing it. Now if that is the situation

then it is almost impossible to get a majority of voters in a majority of states. The party system is what has made passing things very difficult because there are very few occasions when all sides will support the one issue as they did in 1967. So it does seem to me that there is a problem. If you ever taught the Constitution, as I have done, and gone through it, there is a great deal which simply no longer really has any relevance and there are enormously important things that are not there. It really is a document that should be profoundly changed. But how that is done, I think, is almost impossible to suggest."

The Williams paper then continues to examine whether or not Andrew Inglis Clark was the 'primary architect' of the Constitution. This aspect, who were the architects of the Constitution of 1901, is of considerable interest to Australian constitutional lawyers but less relevant to today's issues. Briefly, this question was dealt with as follows by Williams:

"The Constitution was written at the 1897–98 Federal Convention (the second Convention) by delegates from five colonies—a total of 54 men, only 17 of whom had been at the 1891 Convention. Most significantly, the majority was popularly elected. They were representatives. Unlike the appointed members of the 1891 Convention, they represented the Australian voters. This fact influenced their approach. The delegates at this Convention unambiguously affirmed that their work was to be their own—that it was neither their role nor their intention to follow the 1891 constitution bill. Indeed, on the opening day of the second Convention, Edmund Barton, the Convention leader, declared that, 'while ... a great deal of instruction may be derived from the Bill of 1891, the business of this Convention is to arrive at a conclusion, not under the influence of the previous work, but by its own efforts.'"

Roles of the Convention Participants

Several other politicians and judges contributed to the final draft after the three Conventions held in 1897 and 1898, among them Charles Cameron Kingston, a South Australian politician, who had also written a draft in 1891, and the Chair of that meeting, Queensland Chief Justice Sir Samuel

Griffith. Politicians like the NSW Premier Henry Parkes, who had called for federation at the so-called Tenterfield Oration in 1889, and Edmond Barton, a NSW politician and later Australia's first (Protectionist) Prime Minister, also contributed. Kingston formed a contrast to Clark in several ways. He favoured the Westminster practice that Ministers should be members of parliament, was not as taken with the US model as Clark was, and supported a weaker federal government. Importantly, he contributed clauses on industrial relations e.g. the influential arbitration power. Surprisingly, Clark was not a formal delegate at the 1897/8 Convention.

Williams argued:

> *"The recent interest in Inglis Clark stems from his relevance to contemporary debates. His perceived republican sympathies and discussion of constitutional interpretative methods has meant that his scholarship can be analyzed in ways that are directly relevant to Australia. When Justice Deane famously described Inglis Clark as 'the primary architect of our Constitution' it was in the context of a sophisticated debate about how the Australian Constitution should be interpreted to meet the challenges of modern Australia. He was advancing his jurisprudential approach to the Constitution when he stated:*
>
> *'The present legitimacy of the Constitution as the compact and highest law of our nation lies exclusively in the original adoption (by referenda) and subsequent maintenance (by acquiescence) of its provisions by the people. While they remain unaltered, it is the duty of the courts to observe and apply those provisions, including the implications which are legitimately to be drawn from their express terms or from the fundamental doctrines which they incorporate and implement ... Moreover, to construe the Constitution on the basis that the dead hands of those who framed it reached from their graves to negate or constrict the natural implications of its express provisions or fundamental doctrines would deprive what was intended to be a living instrument of its vitality and its adaptability to serve succeeding generations. Indeed, those errors of such a dead hands theory of construction were made plain by Inglis Clark in explaining why the Constitution was 'to be construed as having reference to varying*

circumstances and events.' Thus Inglis Clark's relevance is not as some long since dead framer, but as an important standard bearer in a fundamental debate about how our Constitution is to be interpreted."

Unfortunately, there is clearly widespread agreement that there is a limit to the capacity for interpretation. The plain fact that amendment of the Constitution has been virtually impossible due to the adversarial party system and the complex provisions of Section 128, has presented Australia with a massive constitutional dilemma. The constitutional power has shifted increasingly to the power of interpretation by High Court judges. In a financial sense the power has shifted very significantly to the federal government. The imbalance is grotesque. Certainly, Clark himself stressed the need for flexibility in the federal Constitution to adapt to changing circumstances and events but this has proved impossible for a very long time. It would be completely foolhardy to continue with a set of ground rules that is clearly out of touch with the society it is meant to serve. We should also consider some other realities here that are often overlooked in this kind of debate.

First of all there actually are major differences between the US and Australian Constitutions. The strong executive position of the US President was not adopted here. The US Constitution is a solid statement of Independence of the American people having sent the Brits home in 1776. The 1901 Constitution Act of Australia is an Act of the British Parliament. In the 1787 US Constitution there is an extensive Bill of Rights of the people deliberately avoided in Australia. The US political Executive is entirely outside the Legislature, it is extra-parliamentary. There is a clear separation of Executive and Legislature. In Australia the Westminster practices apply. Cabinet Ministers have to be in and of the Parliament and they dominate the legislature.

The Australian Constitution was approved by delegates voted in by systems of limited franchise: Women, the Indigenous people and Territorians did not have the vote. Voting was voluntary. In the final constitutional referendum in the six states the turnout average was around 56%, the average majority percentage was approximately 68%.

Federation was undoubtedly quite an achievement, in terms of bundling economic and strategic interests, both imperial and local. However, the federal arrangement to bind six British colonies into one political unit was in fact a political bargain that suited the circumstances of the period and the environment. As a nation building exercise it was only a first step on the long road to an existence as a sovereign nation. Given that it could hardly be updated since one wonders how some can argue that it is still suited to a vastly different, multi-cultural society served by modern communications and transport modes.

Geoffrey Robertson (2012) has written a scathing assessment of 1901 in a recent text. In the light of the current desire of Attorney-General Senator George Brandis to legalize expressing bigotry in some way it is interesting to consider the progress or otherwise since 1901:

> *"If I am a refugee from anything, it is from the Australian constitution, or at least from having to spend my time in court in arid argument over a constitutional law that is mainly about allocation of power between federal and state governments. Australians – or at least the Australian – react with mindless patriotism whenever 'our constitution' is said to need updating. It is necessary to remind them, in this case in a Bulletin edition celebrating in 2001 the centenary of Federation, of the virulence of the racism of the time, which ensured that human rights were absent from a document agreed at a referendum from which women, Blacks and territorians were excluded. It is anachronistic to see the Australian constitution in any true sense as the work of Australians: it was the work, more accurately, of unevolved Australians, who were hooked intravenously to British blood. And in the class-calcified Britain of Queen Victoria, where small children were put up chimneys and down mines, there was no talk of human rights."*

To the question "when did Australia become an Independent nation?" he gave seven answers in his 2009 book The Statute of Liberty. This is the list (restated in 2012):

> *1901: the year of federation, but this was far from real independence.*

1931: The Statute of Westminster, another Act of Parliament following the "Balfour Declaration"

1939: that Statute of Westminster Adoption Act, passed in 1942 by the Australian Parliament, backdated to September 1939, on which day the Australian government felt itself bound by the British declaration of war on Germany.

1941: Declaration of War on Japan. The Curtin Government acted on its own initiative.

1942 : The Act removed doubts about the validity of Australian laws, but it did not apply to the states.

The Australia Acts, 1986 – seven laws enacted by the states, the British Government and finally by the Commonwealth government severed the constitutional tie to Britain. However, the British monarch remained as Australia's head of state, the Queen of Australia.

So, independent? "Not yet", Robertson claims, "because the constitution remains part of British law. The British Parliament's The Commonwealth of Australia Constitution Act 1900, although the source of federal power, is now the Australian Constitution, which can pursuant to section 128 be amended or replaced by the Australian people voting in a referendum.

So, Robertson wrote,

"Until Australia decides to adopt a brand new constitution, or at least amends the present document to establish a Republic, the source of federal power remains the UK parliament."

In the 1890s the six colonies had a good deal of colonial autonomy, some of which they surrendered to a federal government in 1901 for the sake of unity of purpose, and promoting inter-state trade and security. However, 114 years later this state autonomy has been steadily eroded. We now hear several politics professors saying that:

"Australia is no longer a true federation because the states have lost their true sovereignty" (Wiltshire, 2008).

Former WA Premier Carmen Lawrence, at a Constitution Day in Canberra in 2010, claimed that:

"The Australian community seems increasingly to hold the view that the states in their current form do not perform a useful role and the Federation requires a major overhaul."

In recent years, opinion polls show the growing desire to abolish the states and to introduce a system of governance that promotes effective decentralization. What Federation achieved in 1901 is now part of political history. It is a construct no longer viable for the greatly changed circumstances. Turning the clock back in some way is no option.

Obviously, Clark was a remarkable theorist, politician, judge and scholar. Regrettably, his advocacy for proportional representation, a much more democratic electoral system than systems based on single-member districts, was not discussed at all at this conference. It is an adaptation of a little used British system devised by Thomas Hare in the mid-19th century, and became known as the Hare-Clark system. It was devised prior to the emergence of mass political parties or adult suffrage. It has been used in Tasmania's lower house, since 1907, in a number of state Upper Houses and the ACT. It is suitable for small chambers and local elections in which individual candidates are preferred by electors. However, this is not the system of proportional representation that is used in most other countries; these are based on party lists. Party list systems are much more effective and simpler than Hare-Clark, for voters, parties and electoral commissions. Australia's dominant electoral system, anchored in the 1918 and 1924 Commonwealth Electoral Acts, has produced the adversarial two-party system, which has contributed greatly to the lack of success in achieving constitutional amendments in Australia.

Chapter 10

Give Pollies a Chance

David Bofinger

Australia's system of federalism causes it a good deal of unnecessary trouble, and the problems are largely caused by the constitutionally guaranteed semi-independence of the states. The Constitution reserves many important government functions to the states, and these are often important functions like health and policing. The national government gains some influence through control of the money or abuse of its power to regulate corporations, but each state is largely free to develop entirely parallel systems intended to perform almost exactly the same functions. States also compete against each other for foreign investment. The result is greatly increased rent-seeking behaviour and costs of administration.

I won't try to prove this thesis here; instead I recommend Mark Drummond's analysis. But supposing we accept it, and want to modify the Constitution to ameliorate the problem, there are at least two approaches we might try.

The remedy more commonly discussed, both in this book and by proponents generally, is to rewrite the Constitution to create a system of government not subject to these problems. The general theme here is that a state is too large an organization to be responsible for implementation of government, but too small to be efficiently responsible for policy and legislation. States are therefore, abolished. Policy and legislative responsibilities are moved up to the national level of government. Implementation responsibilities are moved down to a new level I will call regions, perhaps new creations or perhaps strengthened local government. The regions serve the duties of the administrative areas already used by state governments for such functions as health and policing. The advantage over using such areas is that the subnational units, having their own elected officials, are more democratically accountable than centrally appointed boards. They would also be more horizontally integrated, with the same authority responsible for implementation of multiple governmental functions: this could be good or bad.

While this would potentially be a great improvement there are issues with this approach. First, it requires us to come up with a specific model that solves these problems without creating too large and serious a batch of new ones. Then we have to get it accepted. Each of these will require a great deal of debate and analysis.

Even when we have done all that, if the regional boundaries and powers are constitutionally defined, the way states are and as they are in most proposals, then we will still have a system that is difficult to change. Regional boundaries chosen before the change may prove to be mistakes, and even the good decisions will get less sensible as Australia evolves, but fixing them still requires a referendum. New responsibilities will appear, the way television and the internet did under the present Constitution, and will not necessarily fall under the purview of the level of government best qualified to handle them.

Finally, such a proposal requires us to place a good deal of faith in regional governments that will either be entirely new creations or radically changed from anything Australia has seen before. Since the local government level presently receives the least attention from the media and voters, it has been more free than the Commonwealth or states to become corrupt.

So if making a new system of governance is so difficult, the obvious next question is whether there are any mechanisms around that might do some of the work for us. What we need is a supply of talented and motivated people, with knowledge and experience relevant to the work, and some structure that can yoke them into a team. Preferably they should meet and debate frequently, so they can implement changes as quickly or slowly as seems wise at the time. And they should be strongly scrutinized by the media and voters.

We have such a group and it's called federal parliament. Whatever mockery our representatives get or deserve, and surely there's a great deal of both, federal politicians are mostly smart people experienced in addressing these sorts of problems. To prove their motivation they have chosen a vocation with taxing hours, appalling job security and a vicious substitute for a recruitment interview, and if they are not exactly poor then most of them could probably make a lot more doing any of several different things. Being politicians has forced them to work with people despite ideological disagreement or personal dislike. They have democratic accountability built into their selection criteria and the close attention paid them by the media, and these have probably weeded out most of the worst of them. They're a long way from perfect, but they are far and away the most qualified people we have to run such a project.

A common concern typically raised at this point is that the Commonwealth, if not balanced by the states, will grow too strong. There are two versions of this argument.

The first fears tyranny, valuing the states as a bulwark against a dictatorship of the Commonwealth. We have a laboratory for testing this argument, by comparing federal and non-federal states (Australia, Canada, Great Britain, New Zealand and the United States, for instance) that are otherwise very similar to Australia and each other. The lack of strong protection for states doesn't seem to imperil democracy in these cases: New Zealand and Britain do not seem to be particularly more or less democratic than Australia and the United States. So I'm skeptical of this argument.

The other argument is from efficiency. There is a tendency for any organization that can control something to exercise that power. This isn't entirely an aspect of megalomania, to some extent it derives from Wilsonian principles of responsibility and a reluctance to look indifferent. If a national government is providing money for, say, roof insulation it will probably feel obliged to closely monitor how that money is spent. Even if the body best placed to administer the program is at a much lower level they will be required to fill in forms justifying how they spent their Commonwealth patron's money. And should the Commonwealth not keep close oversight on the program it will be criticized for it, the moment it runs into difficulty (or tragedy). This leads to over-centralisation.

Over-centralization is certainly a problem, but it's unclear the states are a good way to stop it. The states have to fill in a lot of paperwork for the Commonwealth. The Commonwealth is forced to deal with them but they need its money, so the reporting issue still exists. I've tried to add some anti-centralizing mechanisms in my proposals below.

So let's consider how we might, instead of bypassing the normal political processes, harness them to dissolving some of the state-based obstacles to reform of governance. The main problem with the status quo is that the obstacles are so strong it's impractical for Commonwealth politicians to make substantial changes. The Commonwealth can cajole or bribe, to some extent it can threaten, but a state that digs its heels in is practically impossible to dislodge, especially without ruining the lives of its citizens. What if we breached some of those obstacles, and sent our politicians in to see what they could do? Might they come up with a better system of governance?

I'm sure many of my readers feel they wouldn't. They may be right. But I do believe the politicians deserve a chance, and so far they haven't had one because the barriers have been too strong. Those barriers - elements of the Australian Constitution that protect the right of states to govern - can be divided into several categories. Each category defends states against one way in which their powers might be eroded.

The first category is definitions of the powers of the Commonwealth and the states: Section 51, which lists the subjects on which both states and the Commonwealth can legislate, and Section 52, which lists subjects on which only the Commonwealth can legislate. Changing either of these presently requires a referendum. In the absence of these protections, the Commonwealth's ability to override state legislation, given to it in Section 109, would be very powerful.

The second category is protections for the existence of states, and of their autonomy. The most important is Section 106, which says state constitutions persist and Section 107, which says the powers of the state parliaments persist. There's also Section 108, which says state laws persist, and Section 118, which requires the Commonwealth to give full faith and credit to state laws, records and judgments. In principle, removing these might weaken the states but it would also create a legal vacuum: it's almost certainly not a good way to attack the problem.

A third category allows for changes in the borders of states, the creation of new states, etc. Section 111 allows states to surrender territory to the Commonwealth, Sections 121 and 124 allow the Commonwealth to create new states, and Section 123 allows state borders to be changed. The defence for states here is that any action affecting a state requires the consent of the state parliament.

A fourth category dictates that state of residence of a voter will affect the voter's power over the Commonwealth. Sections 7 and 24 provide greater Commonwealth parliamentary representation to smaller states. Section 128 requires referendums to receive not just a majority of voters, but a majority of voters in a majority of states, and a majority of voters in any state affected in particular ways.

Of these four categories the last is the odd one out. It is the only one to concern itself with the power of voters rather than of parliaments. It is also the only one that creates a barrier internal to the Commonwealth rather than external to it: the Commonwealth is not prevented from taking actions but rather its own decision-making procedures are influenced on a state basis. A case can certainly be made for reforming the sections of Category Four: the inflated representation of Tasmania is an absurd violation of the one-vote-one-value principle; justifications rely on the belief that the states define one of the most important communities of interest in the country, which is far from clear. It's hard to believe anything similar would be adopted if we were writing a constitution today *ab initio*. On the other hand, in our modern party-based political regime the difference between the voting of a member of parliament elected by Tasmanian voters and one elected by New South Welsh voters is probably not huge, and more due to the Hare-Clarke electoral system than anything else. So the artificial profusion of Tasmanian senators may not be doing all that much harm. I won't speak more on Category Four, which is really the subject of a quite different essay.

The other three categories all limit the powers of the national parliament, effectively requiring the consent of state parliaments before taking some kinds of actions. For protection of the states all these categories are needed and almost any breach in them leads to states that can be crippled by national parliament. Removal of the Category One protection, for example, permitting the Commonwealth to add entries to Section 52, would allow the Commonwealth parliament to make states powerless irrelevancies without portfolio. Removal of the Category Two protection would allow the Commonwealth to take over states from the inside, by modifying the state constitution. Removal of the Category Three protection would allow the Commonwealth to deprive the states of their territory. Only with all three in place are the states protected in, respectively, their authority, soul and body.

Anyone who believes in state rights can stop here and take my essay as a defence of the status quo. For those of us who believe state independence should be weakened, the question now becomes which protection would be best to weaken, and how. Unfortunately removing or weakening one of the types of protection, while it would seriously reduce the independence of the states, is probably not the path to good governance. This at a minimum should include democratic accountability and efficiency. The principle of subsidiarity, that a program should be administered at the lowest practical level, may be of use here.

Part of the problem with weakening only one protection is that if the Commonwealth has only one tool in their kit they will be both tempted and forced to use it wherever they want reform, regardless of whether it is the best mechanism. Weakening the first protection, for example, while leaving the second and third intact, leaves us with states that have fewer responsibilities but continue to control the same areas. In the extreme case, where all powers are taken from them, they become zombie organizations, social clubs or (at best) discussion circles. If some powers are left to them then those powers will continue to be exercised along borders written in the nineteenth century.

Eliminating only the second protection allows states to be taken over from inside. States might then be operated by the Commonwealth as puppets, retaining their de facto existence only at the Commonwealth's pleasure. But such a solution should surely raise some eyebrows from a democracy point of view and without the ability to modify the list of powers of the Commonwealth we must doubt if it's even legal for the Commonwealth to become the de facto government in these areas.

Similarly, weakening the third protection would allow new states to be abolished and created more easily. But if the other two protections are intact then the country would then have to be governed either by new states with similar powers (which would probably not be very efficient) or directly by the Commonwealth (which would probably not be very democratic).

In practice the government will probably work better if there's some weakening in multiple areas. So how much weakening do we need? This is a very difficult question to answer. We want the sub-national governments--be they states, regions, local governments, something else or a mix of the above--to be sufficiently independent that their leaders can go to elections with some confidence of being able to do what they promise. We don't want the national government to micromanage them or for there to be a lot of reporting requirements to administer. But we want the sub-nationals sufficiently subordinated that they can be forced to cohere to policy and legislation created at the national level. This is a difficult balancing act, with reporting being perhaps the hardest part of the problem.

What follows is a suggestion for how we might weaken the protections. It's not intended to be prescriptive, just an example system plucked from among the large range of reasonable options. I hope it illustrates some of what I see as the principles that should drive such decisions. We want to make it hard for a government of the day to over-centralize power, yet make it possible for power to be moved upward from the sub-national governments to the national government. A possible mechanism would be to make it easier to transfer power from the national government down to the sub-national ones than it is to move it up, and I've included that in my proposal.

Here are some changes that could be used to weaken the states, relative to the Commonwealth.

Easier changes to the powers of the Commonwealth:

A power can be added to Section 51, added to Section 52 or moved from Section 51 to Section 52 by a three-quarters vote of each house of the Commonwealth parliament. A power can be deleted from Section 51, deleted from Section 52 or moved from Section 52 to Section 51 by a simple majority vote of each house of parliament. This would allow the commonwealth to take over powers from the state or (more easily) to devolve powers back to the states. In practice, I hope and believe, the Commonwealth would take over more of the legislative and policy aspects of government while leaving more of the administrative responsibilities in the hands of the states. It might be appropriate to explicitly recognize that distinction in the Constitution, though I'm not sure how. The referendum mechanism should be left intact as an alternate path, though we would not expect it to be used very often.

States subordinate to Commonwealth:

Section 106 could be modified to allow a state constitution to be changed by a three-quarters vote of each house of the Commonwealth parliament. Among other applications this would allow states to be effectively abolished when they aren't needed.

State parliaments can be overridden:

Sections 111, 123 and 124 could be modified so that a three-quarters vote of each house of the Commonwealth parliament is a substitute for the consent of a state parliament. This would allow state borders to be changed and new states created.

Encouragement of one vote, one value:

Sections 7, 24, 121, 122 and 124 could be modified to encourage a one-vote, one-value principle. A three-quarters vote of each house of the

Commonwealth parliament would suffice to reduce an original state's senatorial representation below the usual minimum, provided the number of senators per elector after the reduction is still at least the national average. A three-quarters vote of each house of the Commonwealth parliament would suffice to reduce an original state's House of Representatives representation below the usual minimum (i.e. five) provided the number of members per elector after the reduction is still at least the national average. Sections 121, 122 and 124 could be modified to require that, to the greatest extent possible, any territory or new state must be given senators and members so that its number of senators per elector is within the range of other states and territories, and similarly for the House of Representatives.

Allowing the Commonwealth to change its own constitution like this, even in minor ways, would be a significant change. Much stronger versions of this power are, however, normal for many parliaments, including the British parliament and Australian state parliaments. Ironically, by allowing the parliament to rewrite its own constitution to some extent, these changes make the Commonwealth more closely resemble the states.

I may have erred on the side of caution here. The three-quarter vote is a high hurdle, especially in the last case where the parliament would be reducing representation that most of the time will favour one side or the other. Still, these changes would greatly free up the Commonwealth parliament's hand. And if they work then something more generous could be tried.

The question remains whether such changes would be easier or harder to achieve than a newly written structure would be. Any of these changes would require a referendum. In the present through medium term future Australia will have an adversarial regime, where a referendum can only be expected to pass if it has bilateral support and perhaps not even then. A referendum to make changes resembling the ones I propose will not happen tomorrow, but the same can be said for any new system of governance in Australia.

The best chance this idea has is if a wide variety of reformers are willing to support it, all hoping to lobby for their own system of governance to be adopted by parliament. If the change is presented as making Australia more like Canada, New Zealand or Britain, and less like the United States, it may not seem particularly threatening.

A modification that might make it less threatening still would be to allow such a scheme to be introduced on a state-by-state basis. All the changes above would come into effect in a state only after that state passed irreversible enabling legislation. The hope would be that a few states would lead the way, that their citizens would achieve superior outcomes, and that other states would follow.

Australia has no greater concentration of political power and skill than its Commonwealth parliament. Let's cut off their manacles, and see where they can take us.

Chapter 11

Does Australia's 'Representative Democracy' represent us?

Anthony Nicholas

Summary

The citizens of an indirect democracy such as Australia elect a parliament, which supposedly represents them; it also selects the government. Our parliamentary representation is skewed by the system of governance, comprising the Constitution, the Westminster tradition and some decisions of the parliament. The net result is that we have an imbalance that favours the smaller states, a rigid two-party oligarchy that disadvantages smaller groups, and a male-dominated parliament. A new constitution that creates a representative parliament and a stable national government could remedy these failings.

Geographic representation

The Constitution sets down the allocation to the states of members of the House of Representatives [HoR] and the Senate and gives the parliament power to allocate parliamentary representatives to the territories. The average numbers of voters needed to elect a parliamentarian in each state or territory varies from seventy-six thousand in NSW to twenty-one thousand in Tasmania, constituting a considerable bias toward the less populous states. The allocation formulae for each state provides twelve senators and a minimum of five members in the HoR. These quotas give politicians from the smaller states a disproportionate weight in party-room decision-making. Although considered a reasonable arrangement by the colonies in the 1890s, it has become more unbalanced in the twenty-first century.

In our national parliament, all the citizens of the country should be represented with equal weight. That is to say, members of parliament should be elected by roughly the same number of voters throughout the nation, no matter in which state or territory those voters live. As a national parliament, it should represent the nation.

The biased distribution of voters is shown in Figure 1; it is redolent of the 'rotten boroughs' of nineteenth century England or the gerrymanders of present-day America. Australia deserves better; a future without the straight-jacket of state governments. That future is explored further in Chapter 8, "Governing Without State Governments".

Figure 1   Voters per Commonwealth Parliamentarian

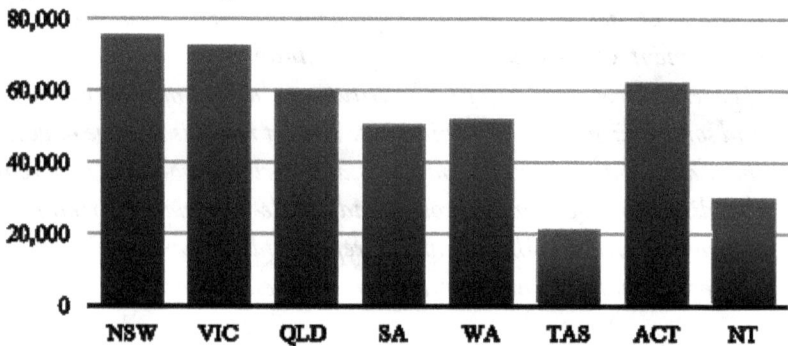

Exclusive Electorates

The traditional Westminster system uses single member electorates, which in eighteenth century Britain, would allow the gentlemen voters to endorse a prominent citizen as a member of parliament. In twenty-first century Australia, each single-member electorate has about sixty times as many voters as in eighteenth century Britain. In addition, we have universal suffrage and a literate population, rather than an exclusive electorate of well-to-do gents. With about 90,000 voters each, single-member electorates strongly favour the two major parties that dominate the political landscape, effectively excluding minor parties. Unless a minor party's support is concentrated in a limited geographical region, it will fail to gather sufficient votes to gain seats. On the other hand, if the support of a successful minor party is based on territorial interests, its members may be out of touch with national affairs. Either way, minor parties fall between the cracks in our existing system.

Figure 2   Commonwealth Seats and Votes

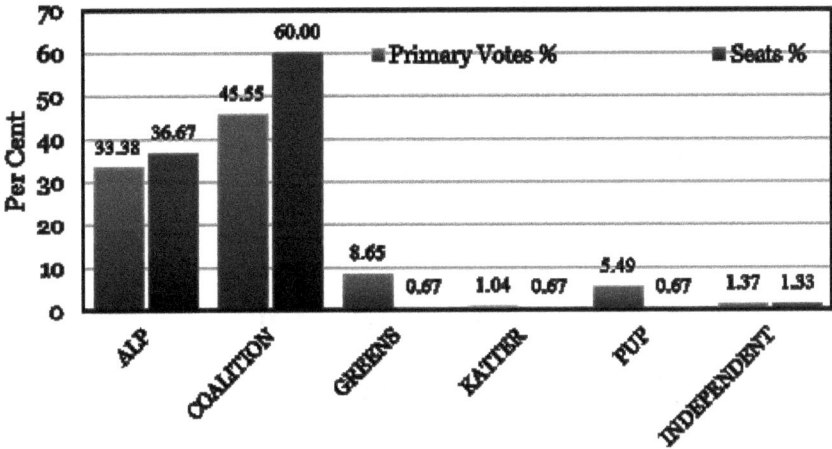

As shown in Figure 2 above, the primary votes in the 2013 HoR election were 45.55% for the government parties, 8.65% Greens and 5.49% Palmer United Party with 33.38% for the ALP and 1.37% independent; but the Greens and the PUP gained only 1.33% of the seats, compared with 90.36% for the major parties. Over one million Greens voters and 0.7 million PUP voters, out of a total of nearly 14 million, returned only one HoR member of each party, the same number as the independents. The major parties more easily reach the quota of 50% in the single-member electorates.

Minorities are important because they add diversity and innovation, while the major parties tend to compete over a limited range of vote-winning issues and then more as adversaries than advocates. Major parties' policies on some prominent issues, such as not to reform the counter-productive drug laws, appear to be tacitly agreed rather than debated, in spite of well known community concerns and potential majority support. An effective modern system of Proportional Representation [PR] would overcome this lopsidedness. A nationally uniform PR system would require constitutional reform to remove the restriction due to state borders. Election outcomes would also become more meaningful with voluntary voting, because a significant proportion of the voting public, who are now forced to vote, have little interest or knowledge of politics and consequently, their votes tend to be determined by the weight of political advertising, rather than a grasp of the issues.

Not many voters have enough knowledge of the candidates to rank more than a few; so the selection or design of a nationally uniform PR system should take account of voters' likely knowledge of candidates. The 'party-list' system of PR, used in most European countries, is a good starting point from which to replace the ludicrous 'single transferable vote' system that is used in Tasmania and the Senate elections.

Women in Parliament

In the twenty-first century, it is a reasonable expectation that the national parliament of an indirect democracy such as Australia would reflect the characteristics of the population, particularly the proportion of women. In the HoR of the 44th parliament women made up 26% of members and in the Senate, 41%. The proportion of women in the parliaments of other countries is presented by the Parliamentary Library. If our parliament is to represent the Australian community, then men and women should be there in equal numbers. The Member for Murray suggests 51% women.

Until well into the twentieth century, it was presumed that males were better equipped than females to run the governments of the world. That view has moderated after two catastrophic world wars, a crippling depression and a global finance crisis that impoverished millions of hard working Americans and others. A balance between the sexes is important because men and women show differences in their interests and their way of thinking; there are many books on the subject.

In our parliaments, men outnumber women, not because they provide better representation, but because they have natural advantages in gaining election. Although it helps, proportional representation does not achieve equality of representation between men and women in more than a few other countries. In Australia, sustained by a system of single-member electorates, our two-party political oligarchy spends much of its energy in adversarial play-acting, a mutually understood ritual in which each side of Australian politics has to be seen fighting the other. This mock combat avoids the constructive discussion of real issues. It also invites, if not demands, the fighting qualities of the Australian male, helping to justify his dominance of the parliament.

In seeking attention from the public and the media, a significant proportion of the male members of the parliament compete with outrageous behaviour. Question time is, to quote the Member for Murray, The Hon. Dr. Sharman Stone, (ABC Q&A, 12 May 2014), *"...the main show for the boys".* This show is also a disgrace to the country and its parliament. Many ordinary citizens, who see 'the show' on TV, are offended by its distortion of the craft of politics; public respect for the political class plummets further as a result.

Our parliaments also tend to be biased toward men's concerns, such as roads and aeroplanes, at the expense of women's interests. Even female oriented initiatives like Mr. Abbott's paid parental leave scheme, appear to miss the major concern of working women, which is probably child care rather than pregnancy. The scheme also denies the basic principle that government welfare is based on need rather than employment contracts. Parliament would not only be more balanced but also more representative of the population, if half the seats in the parliament were reserved for each sex; voters would be invited to vote for equal numbers of men and women.

Remedies

A new constitution would be needed to remedy the three deficiencies described above. Specifically, this constitution would need to disregard state borders and introduce a nationally uniform system of multi-member electorates with equal numbers of seats in parliament reserved for men and women. The concept of the Senate as a states' house should be recognized as outdated; the Senate has not represented the states since the very early years of the federation and is never likely to again.

The outcome would be a unicameral parliament, because there are no realistic factors on which to create the equivalent of another house to replace the Senate. The national parliament should be limited to legislating on issues that require national regulation or coordination, leaving local or regional governments to adapt those laws to local circumstances. Nineteen electorates with twelve seats each – six for women and six for men – could provide adequate diversity with a parliament of 228 seats, compared to its present size of 226 seats (150 in the HoR and 76 in the Senate).

The procedures of the parliament should be structured in such a way that it could not be taken over by any one political ideology, whether in the form of a demagogue or a movement. Probably, the best tactic to forestall such a threat is a program of frequent elections. The current average term between federal elections in Australia is 2 years, 7 months and 11 days, a relatively short period diminished by the turmoil of national elections at each end of the period, which gives the incumbent government little time to govern. This short term of government could not be reduced beneficially.

However, a practice of the corporate world could be borrowed to achieve frequent elections without disruption; board members of public companies are typically elected annually for three-year terms, successively, a few members at a time. In a parliament of nineteen electorates each of twelve seats, successive elections in one electorate at a time, every two months, would see the whole parliament 'turned over' every three years. An election every three months would give members five-year terms. Change in the political balance of the parliament would be gradual with little likelihood of sensation, so elections would become low-key events that would not attract the deluge of misinformation, 'non-core' promises, personal abuse and false expectations that occur under the current system. Elections could even include rational discussion of the important issues, a potentially radical development that would be regarded as progress in some circles.

Periodic non-compulsory elections for one electorate at a time would best be conducted by a postal ballot or for those who prefer it, by the Internet. These elections would not be likely to attract the extravagant and misleading advertising that is occasioned by our current 'winner-takes-all' elections; few donors would bankroll an election every two or three months, particularly if there is little prospect of advantage for them. Taxpayer funding should be limited to the circulation of candidates' presentations enclosed with the voting papers and/or made available on the Internet, thus further reducing the demand for advertising. The potential for propaganda and corruption that arises from 'donations' to party funds would thus be markedly diminished and the idea that campaign advertising should be curtailed by law could probably be put to rest. Taxpayer funding of political parties for election advertising could no longer be justified, if it ever was.

Further, the expense to the taxpayer would be much reduced by the natural efficiency of routine voting procedures that would be in frequent use by the electoral office, instead of having to maintain enough resources to conduct nationwide elections every 2.6 years. Small-scale elections would require only a fraction of the staff and equipment now needed.

The costs and inconvenience of elections would be reduced if voting were conducted by post and/or electronically with polling stations at local government offices as a back up. A national postal-voting election was held in 1998 to elect a Constitutional Convention. It was concluded with a participation rate of 47% and a minimum of fuss, showing that both the voters and the Australian Electoral Commission can cope with postal voting in a national election. There is no doubt that an internet-based voting system could be developed to replace postal voting for voters who prefer it. The net effect of this electoral process would be to create a virtually perpetual parliament that can be seen as a natural extension of the idea of overlapping terms for Senators. The forms of government that could be derived from such a perpetual, representative parliament are discussed in Chapter 13, 'The Westminster Legacy'.

However, there is an ever-present possibility that the parliament will adopt an entrenched position on some matter of popular concern, for example, euthanasia. Citizen initiated referendums can be used to resolve situations of this sort, as in some states of the USA and Switzerland. Voting could be in conjunction with the successive elections for each electorate, by post and voluntary, until the matter of the referendum is decided one way or the other. Quotas for the proportion of the electorate required to express their support for holding a referendum would be required and another quota set for the minimum proportion of the total population voting in favour of a proposition before it would be accepted as law.

Conclusion

A new constitution without state borders is required to remove the constraints on representative democracy that are identified above and to introduce citizen-initiated referendums. Due to the Westminster tradition, our community enjoys most of the precious qualities of democracy: freedom of speech, communication and movement, as well as separation of the justice system from the executive government, the rule of law and a largely apolitical public service. But, our governance is dangerously close to oligarchy because government is in the hands of the two powerful political groups that comprise only a small number of participants.

The cause of achieving representative democracy could be advanced by the preliminary step of introducing PR in the House of Representatives within the existing constraints of the Constitution. An alternative re-arrangement of electorates could be to join existing electorates in pairs to elect one woman and one man. The odd numbers of seats would leave one seat spare in each state, which could be assigned to a man or a women according to the ratio of women to men in each state.

Chapter 12

Reforming Australia's Governance

Summary of other proposed models

Jim Snow

Contents

1. Introduction

This chapter covers options for reform of Australia's governance. Some options dealt with in other chapters are mentioned; others not so dealt with are summarised here. Beyond Federation participants have deliberately avoided seeking the general endorsement by the group of any particular model and offer them into the arenas of public discussion and research on the political system.

There is one common message in all the proposals: that Australia would be well served by removing state governments and boundaries established under compromises by Australia's early colonial leaders, then ratified in Australia's constitution passed by the parliament of the United Kingdom under Queen Victoria.

The options and models vary from a full re-write of Australia's constitution to specific changes. Some changes suggest a new federal system with local law-making. Others plan unitary government with one parliament while avoiding 'rule from the top'. All endeavour to minimise the growth of parochialism and abuses seen under the planning and other administration of the states. Most changes require at least some degree of constitutional reform.

All the options allow savings for businesses, citizens, occupations and organisations across Australia, leaving funds for tax deductions and worthwhile infrastructure, social and environmental development. The reduction in reporting to the government, fewer regressive taxes and removal of inappropriate state boundaries and nationwide licensing and registration brings more efficiency to government. Democracy would benefit from easier, faster, less confusing and better understood decisions. Criminal, corporate and many other laws would be uniform with appropriate local options through by-laws and fewer over-lapping services.

The reader can judge the ability of each option or model to deal with many other important policy questions including: Does the proposal improve government efficiency and bring down the cost of government? To what extent does it increase local innovation and motivate local communities to gain social, economic and environmental benefit? To what extent does it counter excessive 'rule from the top'? On the other hand is there a sufficient national perspective to discourage parochialism? Will the proposal combat corruptive tendencies evident in state-based planning, development and other decisions? Will change respond positively to the growing tendency of electors to reject the political parties? Will the change allow stable government? Where there is conflict between some aims can a worthwhile balance be achieved?

2. Options for Change

Constitutional reform is the subject of many other chapters in this e-book. After 100 years of trying to get federation right, the editor of this book, former Associate Professor Dr Klaas Woldring said,

> *"Attempts at collaborative federalism have been made before and the problems have only grown*[1] *...Federation is essentially a power bargain that is then written up in a constitution. The power relationships change over time, for all kinds of reasons, but the written constitution can drag behind, as it has in Australia.*

In line with the apparent wish of the original founders that the Constitution would adapt to the times, the planner Dr Geoff Armstrong suggested constitutional provision for a 'use-by date' in a new constitution. He recommended 33 years, but no more than 50 years from its adoption, for a review to be conducted by a political panel required to engage in nation-wide discussion, and finally a referendum. He also suggests making provision for citizen initiated referendums.

3. Constitutional Reform

Local councils and one national government

This model is also discussed in Chapter 8, "Governing without State Governments".

The two most discussed systems are dealt with in separate chapters in this e book - 'Shed-a-Tier' by former Berrigan NSW councillor, Max Bradley and the 'Australia United Plan' by Dr Mark Drummond[2] (see Appendix II of this book, pages 163-6), Convenor of Beyond Federation. Both accept unitary government involving a local government (council) sector and a national sector. Another model by Anthony Nicholas proposes a two-tier system, a national parliament undertaking tasks that require national regulation and local governments collaborating to do the rest. A unicameral national parliament of about twenty electorates returning six female and six male members each would be elected by a modern proportional representation system. Such a parliament would probably displace the two-party oligarchy that compromises our democracy now. A small government of seven to ten ministers, elected from the parliament by proportional representation would comprise a cooperative executive representing the major interest groups in the parliament, perhaps half a dozen different parties. Policies would therefore tend to be balanced, achieving prompt, agreed positions; stable government would prevail, rather than a succession of decisions that lurch from one extreme to another, as happens now with our adversarial regimen. The parliament itself would monitor, review and correct the government, thus performing a constructive role instead of a destructive opposition. Local governments would undertake subnational tasks, collaborating where necessary.

A regional and a national sector

Support for the regional option

Apart from models summarised below the regional-national option has been supported by many people and organisations including the author Rodney Hall and the Business Council of Australia (BCA). The BCA called for restructuring of government in the interest of less overlapping in education, housing, transport and health, better coordination of regulations and action on the mismatch between spending and revenue raising by different governments. It called for a complete reorganisation of the three tier system of government, adding:

"There is a strong case for a small, powerfully coordinating and strategy setting central government supported by a network of regional governments." [3]

The author Rodney Hall used figures by Drummond and data from the BCA to indicate that 60 governments of the style of the Australian Capital Territory (ACT) around the whole nation would bring cost savings of $6.8 billion and 30 of that type would increase the saving to $23.2 billion. Hall said that regional governments would 'probably lie somewhere between the ACT Assembly and the Brisbane City Council in terms of their roles and responsibilities and the populations they serve' [4]. Ray Brownlee, an accountant, in his book *'Vision of a New Society,'* advocated 40 regions. The following are summaries of models discussed by Beyond Federation:

The Hurford Model[5]

Summarised from Drummond's Costing Constitutional Change:

The former Hawke government Minister, Chris Hurford, proposed a federation of 51 regions based on 'community of interest, existing state and federally funded regional areas, biogeographic features such as water catchments and existing associations of local government shires and councils'.

With the states 'not now very close to the people' Hurford aimed for a distribution of public functions between the Commonwealth and the regions according to the 'principles of subsidiarity'...that is the principle that regional governments, which are closer to the people, have the right to perform those functions for which they have competence in their own area. The checks and balances preventing 'tyranny and factionalism' would come from that appropriate allocation of functions.

Each elected member of the regional assembly would be responsible for local services in his or her own electorate and would be advised by a local advisory committee along the lines of parish councils in the United Kingdom. Separate planning divisions should be established in large regions so that no planning division is greater than one million people.

The Ken Thomas Models[6]

Summarised from Drummond's Costing Constitutional Change:

Ken Thomas, founder of TNT (Thomas Nationwide Transport) developed two models and this summarises his second, revised model.

No constitutions

Rule of law grounded in English and Australian statutes to apply

37 region states

The original principles of States Rights as envisaged in the Australian Constitution to apply to those region states

One sovereign House of Parliament, the SENATE, consisting of two senators elected by and from the REGION STATES and with a number of votes to be in ratio to the number of electors the Senator represents

No State or Territory governments or parliaments and no House of Representatives.

Approximately 900 local councils and shires

The Mollison Model

Contributed by Charles Mollison[7]

Any new Constitution must be aimed fairly and squarely at what is wrong with our current one. The system of government we now endure is totally dysfunctional and desperately needs fixing if Australia is to fulfil its potential in the twenty first century. There are many other aspects of our society that a new Constitution could fix but for now, let us concentrate on the system of government.

The primary dysfunctions are:

Lack of accountability. At all three levels, the People have little or no power to hold their "representatives" to account. The only power the Citizens of Australia can wield is to vote one mob out and the other mob in every three or four years. When coupled with huge electorates in which representatives can't talk to their constituents and voters can't talk to their "representatives"; an embedded culture of "party loyalty"; and no power to recall an unsatisfactory representative; we have a situation in which a "government" can do pretty much what it likes while in power including breaking "promises" made during an election.

The electoral system. Currently, *political parties* get to preselect 80%-90% of the candidates. Consequently, our parliaments consist of representatives of political parties – not representatives of communities. "Big Bang" elections result in a lurch to one side or other of the political spectrum causing chaos and confusion, huge losses by business and lack of continuity in public policy.

Adversarial attitudes. The division of our parliaments into "government" and "opposition" under the Westminster system coupled with bi-cameral parliaments leads to poor outcomes or, in extreme cases, no outcomes. Constructive debate has almost disappeared in a culture of partisan point scoring; and more than half our representatives are sidelined as back-benchers or (even worse) opposition back-benchers.

Lack of Separation of Powers. A principle of democratic government is a separation of powers between the Legislature, the Executive and the Judiciary. Our current system totally abrogates this principle by mandating that each Minister (the Executive) is embedded in the Legislature. This also seriously inhibits constructive debate in our parliaments.

Last but not least, we have **far too many elected representatives** and bureaucrats for a population of 24 million people.

There are many other dysfunctional aspects of our current system but if we can devise a system to address these five issues, we will have a much more efficient and effective system of government.

Firstly, to achieve accountability it would be a simple matter to give voters the right to recall an unsatisfactory representative and hold a fresh election. If this provision is coupled with a requirement for the votes on each issue by each representative in our parliaments to be recorded and published; I predict an immediate improvement in communication between representatives and their constituents. However, this would also need much smaller electorates than the 85,000 voters that is the current benchmark for a Federal electorate.

It seems to me that electorates of 5000 voters would achieve the above. However, under the current system that would lead to huge, unwieldy parliaments. However, if we adopt these electorates for a second tier of government (let's call them Regional Assemblies), we could have approximately 100 Regions of a size that would be more viable than many current local Councils. These Regions should not be "one size fits all". A Region of 250,000 Citizens in the major metropolitan areas would retain a sense of community and would yield an "Assembly" of fifty representatives. However, in sparsely populated areas, a Region of 250,000 would be a huge land area and would not be practical. I suggest a minimum of 30,000 citizens in country regions.

Now, if each of those Regional Assemblies were to appoint one of their elected Members to represent their region in a National Parliament, we would have much more equitable representation than we have currently with the Senate.

And, if each of those regional representatives was required to sit in their Regional Assembly one week in four to brief and be briefed; and to conduct a debate of Bills before the National Parliament, the Regional Assemblies would become 100 "Houses of Review" and we would not need a Senate.

Furthermore, we would not need State or Territory Governments, or local Councils. We could have a National Parliament responsible for national policy; and about 100 Regional Assemblies responsible for the delivery of public services; and each could have a rational, definitive allocation of powers and responsibilities in a new Constitution so there is no duplication.

Regional Assemblies would be keen to have their best advocate in the National Parliament and would not be interested in party politics. Furthermore, the 5000 voters in each electorate would be able to know their candidates and would select the best with much less influence of political parties.

Currently, we have very powerful public servants heading up government departments. They have control of all the resources and the advantage of long incumbency. Consequently, they wield all the power but shoulder no ultimate responsibility because, under the Westminster system, it is the Minister who is "responsible". We should do away with "Ministers" and make the Heads of Government Departments responsible for implementing the policies decided by the whole of the National Parliament. That is, they become the "Executive". Thus, we would not divide our Parliament into "government" and "opposition"; all Members of Parliament could sit in "round-table" configuration and have equal say in debates. We could also require a 75% majority for the passage of legislation.

So, with these simple moves, we achieve accountability, eliminate the adversarial culture, reduce the influence of political parties, and regain constructive debate in our Parliaments. We achieve a separation of powers, reduce the number of elected representatives, and, by eliminating one tier of government we reduce the number of bureaucrats. And if we introduced a system whereby each Region appointed their representative in the National Parliament at a different time, we would avoid the effect of the highly disruptive "big-bang" elections we currently endure.

A national sector with either a locally based or a regional sector

The Snow Model[8] (Shared government)

Shared Government brings local or regional government into the Senate of the national parliament so that the Senate loses its responsibility as a house of the states and becomes the house of the regions. Senators are appointed to both the Senate and regional or local government bodies. The House of Representatives continues to form the government in this arrangement.

There is no suggestion that the membership of either house would need to change from the present 76 Senators and approximately 150 members of the House of Representatives. States could remain for non-government and other arrangements where appropriate (for example sporting contests) but state governments and parliaments would go.

The current arrangements allowing joint sittings of both houses of parliament would be broadened to cover all disagreements between the two houses, including budgets, in a combined debate and vote. Although the House of Representatives outnumbers the local sector's Senate the latter is given unprecedented strength and ability to advance communities. The table below shows two ways of bringing the local and national sectors together in income, expenditure and legislative decision making.

The local sector would be based on either local councils or regional (or territory) congresses. Both alternatives elect a number of Senators based on an upper limit for metropolitan cities and a minimum for remote non-metropolitan areas. This removes the current weighting in favour of states and gives a weighting in favour of non-metropolitan regions across the mainland and Tasmania instead of smaller states. Both the alternatives in the table below reject appointment of delegates by regions to the national parliament; a similar proposal to appoint state delegates to the parliament was rejected by the constitutional founders.

The Alternatives

Local councils as the local sector	Regional congresses as the local sector
Local councils as now under one national parliament.	Approximately 27 regions. Perth, Adelaide, Melbourne, Sydney and Brisbane comprise five of the regions and each of the remaining regions to include one or more viable and stable population centres. Election in each region to be by proportional representation. Each region has a Congress consisting of
Up to six Senators elected by groups of local government areas to the national parliament who report to all local council meetings on a rostered basis or to regional meetings convened by local councils. The number of Senators for each grouping are determined by the national parliament	

and elected by popular proportional representation.

Groups of councils form regional planning authorities consisting of council appointees and qualified planners (the latter approved by the Senate).

Possible Disadvantages

Possible local parochialism.

Voluntary councillors may mean:

- Difficulty in influencing national decisions (although the Senate improves local power in the nation's parliament).

- Less opportunity for regional expertise, innovation and coordination.

- No change to the assessment of local government public servant recommendations.

Likely advantages:

- The proposal is easily explained.

- Regional planning authorities can check for corruptive tendencies and political party influence leading to planning and development decisions that benefit local regions, communities and the nation.

- Regional planning authorities would better understand the planning and development needs of local communities than would state authorities.

- A board of full time members and up to six Senators elected by the people using proportional representation.

- A Mayor and a Deputy Mayor elected by each local town, suburb and district and provided with an appropriate allowance.

Local precinct committees may be established by the board as well as planning divisions in populations of more than one million.

The Congress board is the day-to-day implementation and decision-making body with agreed powers including over budgets and by-laws. Meetings of the full board are public. The full Congress meets publicly at agreed intervals to discuss and advise the board. Ability to veto board decisions could be considered. Senators are also elected to the board by popular proportional representation.

The Senators attend congress board meetings as well as the Senate in the national parliament.

Possible Disadvantage:

A greater change from the present system than the local council alternative in column 1.

Likely advantages:

- 27 regions could exceed the savings estimated by Hall in 1998 (see Regional Options above).

- Regional Congress boards would be better able than local councils to provide enough checks on corruptive

- By attending local council meetings on a rostered basis Senators can be exposed to public scrutiny and can be ready to argue the local case in the Senate.

- Direct election of the House of Representatives by the people gives those elected the necessary time to monitor public service decisions and to counter parochial pressures in the Senate.

tendencies and political party influence. Environmental, planning, infrastructure development and social development decisions can benefit local regions, communities and the nation.

- Elected Senators, being members of the congress boards, would be continually confronted with the demands and needs of their local areas and political party influence would be reduced. The Senate is a counter to 'big government' tendencies in the House of Representatives.

- Direct election of the House of Representatives by the people gives those elected the necessary time to monitor public service decisions and to counter parochial pressures in the Senate.

- Less centralist with more influence for local communities.

In the event of a rewrite of the constitution other democratic improvements to the voting and electoral arrangements can be considered along with the options and models summarised in this chapter.

Endnotes

1. Klaas Woldring. formerly Southern Cross University at a conference and round table on Australian Federalism – Rescue and Reform organised by Professor AJ Brown, Griffith University.
2. Dr Mark Drummond, 'Costing Constitutional Change: Estimates of the Financial Benefits of New States, Regional Governments, Unification and Related Reforms' Mark Lea Drummond, School of Business and Government, University of Canberra, November 2007.
3. Business Council of Australia: Government in Australia in the 1990s – A Business Perspective pages 47, 48, 53 ISBN 0 909 815 3N
4. Rodney Hall Abolish the States! 1998. The BCA's 1995 report 'Reforming Fiscal

Reform' by Professor Neville Norman showed how savings could be made.

5. Chris. Hurford, Federal Member for Adelaide 1969 to 1987, Minister for Community Services, Minister for Immigration and Ethnic Affairs, Minister Assisting the Treasurer in the Hawke Labor government. See Drummond above Appendix 2B

6. Ken Thomas, founder of TNT (Thomas Nationwide Transport, February 1, 1980, Australian Regional Government Organisations pamphlet; February 1981 Ken Thomas pamphlet. See Drummond above Appendix 2B

7. Lt.Colonel (Ret) Charles Mollison, Chairman, Foundation for National Renewal

8. Member for Eden Monaro 1983 to 1996, Chair, Government Party Room (Caucus)1993 to 1996.

Chapter 13

The Westminster Legacy

Anthony Nicholas

Summary

Australia has inherited from the United Kingdom an undocumented history of civic practice known as the Westminster Tradition and during the last century it has been expanded. Some of this heritage is out of date and should be reformed, but much of it is relevant today and should be respected.

Our Heritage

The various parliaments in Australia were cast in the Westminster mould. This tradition, emanating from turbulent centuries of British parliamentary experience, has given us the democratic foundation of our system of governance. The tradition encompasses an elected parliament with the sole power to legislate, separation of the judicial system from the executive government, an apolitical public service, a bill of rights [in 1689], a body of common law, a standard of honourable behaviour in public office, a set of rules for our parliaments, and other matters. These ideas are not codified in a written constitution; they are a combination of laws and practices developed over a period of time. Taken together, they provide the democratic basis, not only for the constitution of the United Kingdom, but also for the several independent dominions, including Australia. Many of these principles were pioneered in Britain and now are considered essential elements in any modern democratic government. Even so, many commentators equate popular voting with democracy, despite the many examples from around the world demonstrating that merely electing a government is pointless without those other qualities found in the Westminster tradition.

The 1901 Constitution does not mention these historic conventions, but they are an essential part of our governance and jurisprudence; indeed they are at the core of our democratic form of government. The Constitution itself is essentially a power-sharing agreement between the governments of the states and the Commonwealth in accord with the realities of the late nineteenth century. Then, state education systems were struggling to get primary schools to the dispersed communities that needed them, while hospitals and other health services were in the hands of charities or the medical profession. Transport systems were just passing the horse-and-buggy age. Consequently, the sharing of functions between the two tiers of government was based on a radically different set of parameters than if it were to be done now. It was a different world to ours, and so will our world be for our descendants.

The democratic basis of our governance, therefore consists of two parts. One is the mechanism of federation that comprises the Constitution and the other is the un-codified collection of decisions of various British parliaments that collectively comprise the Westminster tradition plus additional elements that have arisen since 1901. We could call these our 'basic laws'. Although originating in the United Kingdom, they do not deny our national independence; we are still a sovereign nation.

Independence

Australia was dependent on the power of the British Empire in 1901; in the First World War, the Australian Imperial Force (AIF) fought for God, King and Empire. But out of their involvement in that dreadful conflict, Australians began to believe that they could do things differently from the British, in their own way. General John Monash epitomized this belief. The idea was given voice by the prime minister of the day, Billy Hughes, at the Versailles Peace Conference, when the future of the former German colonies in the pacific was being discussed. The following quote from Marchant,[1] describes an incident at the conference.

> *"When the future of New Guinea came to the vote, the story goes, (Woodrow) Wilson (President of the USA) supported a Japanese mandate.*

(Billy) Hughes (Prime Minister of Australia) strongly objected. Wilson, worn down by Hughes' persistence eventually conceded, telling him that Australia could have the mandate over New Guinea as long as Australia promised to send in missionaries, one of Wilson's Christian preferences. Hughes is reported to have jumped up, agreeing whole heartedly, informing Wilson that the natives there had not had a good feed of meat for a long time."

Such expressions of Australian nationhood were quite unusual then, and considering subsequent events, timely. Our twenty-first-century prime ministers have not been as willing to risk upsetting the great powers, particularly the USA.

Since WWI and Versailles, the Westminster tradition has been expanded in the Australian context by successive steps toward independence, or lack of dependence, culminating in the Australia Act in 1986. Our Constitution was created as an Act of the Parliament of the United Kingdom, signed into law by Queen Victoria of England in 1900. She was acknowledged 'the Queen of Australia'. Since then, Australia has progressed from a collection of squabbling colonies to a federation of squabbling states. But during that period, it has also come to be recognized as an independent sovereign nation, initially at the Versailles Conference after the first world war, then by the League of Nations in 1920 and subsequently by the Statute of Westminster promulgated in 1927 and ratified in 1931. That statute was finally adopted by the Australian government in 1942, to give it undisputed control over its armed forces. Since 1945, our independence has been confirmed by the United Nations and the process was virtually sealed by the Australia Act in 1986. Any attempt by the Crown to impose its will on Australia would be emphatically rejected, as it was in 1931, when King George V unsuccessfully opposed the appointment of the Australian born Sir Isaac Isaacs as Governor-General.

The extent to which Australians see themselves as compromised by having a foreign head-of-state is a strong contrast to our desire to have a dependent relationship with the United States. Compared with following the Americans into their disastrous wars, the symbolic threads linking us to the Commonwealth of Nations and the British Royals are an imaginary threat to our independence. The Queen of England is undoubtedly head of the Commonwealth of Nations, but the Australian Governor-General, chosen by our PM, is now the nearest person we have to a head-of-state, if we have to have one. As former Prime Minister, Malcolm Fraser said in a speech in 2012,

> *"... as an independent nation we cannot just keep doing ... what America wants. Troops in Darwin, military activities on Cocos Island, our following America into Iraq, staying in Afghanistan, all indicate an unthinking compliance with American policy."*

Fraser has subsequently pointed out in a book published in 2014, that our simplistic faith in the alliance with the US is not in our national interest. Clearly, that faith is a mark of dependence, inappropriate for a sovereign, if adolescent, nation. There can be little doubt that the two-party oligarchy that arises from single-member electorates in the House of Representatives, is an important factor in maintaining this alliance. In an adversarial political system, questioning by either side of the two-party political divide of the US alliance would risk losing too many votes, because the element of fear would be the dominant feature of any subsequent election campaign; imagine the prospect of savage hordes of crazed invaders sweeping through the country without a single American GI to stop them. So the tactics of the major parties are to say nothing and do nothing; we remain a vassal state of the USA.

Another 'no-no' in Australian politics is any sort of adult discussion of the legislation prohibiting certain drugs. The laws on this subject are almost certainly the most counter-productive ever enacted in our country or any other, yet they are accepted by the major parties for the same reason as is the US alliance: it is too hard to defend against 'shock jocks' and deceitful advertising from the other side of politics. The solution to these dilemmas is to establish a mature and cooperative political environment.

Threats to Our Democratic Tradition

Some political behaviour in Australia today appears to be detrimental to our representative democracy; valuable aspects of the Westminster tradition are falling out of favour with contemporary politicians and the highly disciplined, combative regimen of party-politics. Marchant[3] describes

"The Fragile Nature of the Westminster System (thus)

If this arrangement is tampered with or the principles guiding the Westminster System, such as the principle of providing an apolitical public service of experts is changed or cast aside, then the British system of parliamentary democracy, which has evolved over the centuries and is fragile, could be destroyed. It can not be easily recovered."

There is already too much tampering with the Westminster system. Under the guise of protecting national security, the secrecy provisions of recent legislation or regulation are used to protect governments from legitimate criticism. Some state governments are branding individuals as criminals because they are associates or members of certain 'outlaw' organizations. Actions like these could be interpreted as political interference with traditional justice, in defiance of a noble tradition.

Governments are willing to initiate many projects without the unbiased advice available from an apolitical public service. Our national executive government consists of more than thirty ministers and assistant ministers, plus parliamentary secretaries and a sizeable team of chosen advisors. Such governments are overwhelmingly made up well-meaning functional 'amateurs'[4], and quite a few of them come into office ready to launch their own pet solutions to the problems of the nation, for example, Mr. Abbott's Paid Parental Leave scheme. Plutocratic donors to party funds, whose demands are rarely in the public interest, often inspire party policies and programs. The tested techniques of cost/benefit analysis are usually by-passed in these circumstances, because the government is able to appoint politically sympathetic people as public service department heads, who can over-ride the advice of public service experts. Or they can call on trumped-up rules such as 'commercial-in-confidence' to mask the shady deals that have been concocted.

Preserving and Discarding Traditions

A significant question on the issue of constitutional reform is whether the two parts of our constitutional heritage, our basic laws derived from the Westminster tradition, and the Constitution, should remain separate or be combined in a single document.

In this age of legalistic precision, can the valuable aspects of the Westminster legacy be preserved untouched, or do they need to be codified and expressed as simplistic do's and don'ts? On the other hand, perhaps the Westminster tradition can be given new life by reforming the machinery of government that is prescribed in the Constitution, so that our governments are not driven to disregard it by the adversarial quest for power and the satisfaction of the demands of sectional interests.

The Westminster system includes a tradition of conventional behaviour for the workings of parliaments. The rigmarole about the authority of the Crown, the mace, the structure of the parliament, elections and most of the formalities of the parliament are now symbolic historic traditions, many of which are inappropriate for the twenty-first century. It is time that these conventions were adapted to the circumstances of today and to those of the foreseeable future.

The idea that parliament is a place for debate and discussion is one example of an institutional function being lost to the march of progress. A large part of the contemporary parliamentary performance is aimed at media exposure, rather than debating the qualities of proposed legislation or providing informative answers to questions. Debate on the issues of the day is also conducted outside parliament through television, radio and on-line media; some of this debate is abusive and infantile, led by 'shock-jocks' in the media and abusive commentators on the internet, but it can also be insightful and well informed. Until about one hundred years ago, parliament was the place where disputed opinions and policies could be debated, despite the time and effort required to get there. Now, communication has been transformed and the proximity of the communicators is largely irrelevant. The operation of parliament could be conducted efficiently and effectively from all over the country by various electronic technologies instead of the current practices that waste so much time and money. Nostalgia has its place, but not in the government of the country.

It would be valuable to incorporate the use of modern technology into parliament and into a re-written Constitution, while retaining the enlightened guidelines within the Westminster tradition, our basic laws. Most politicians are already familiar with the 'social media' and other web-based systems; systems analysts could easily design a working net-based system of parliamentary deliberation that would provide better value with less stress than the archaic process in use today. In any case, the procedures of parliamentary government will have to be reformed if parliament would regain the respect of the voters and thus improve our democratic status. A constructive start would be to rebuild the benches of our Westminster-style parliaments so that on the possibly rare future occasions when the parliamentary chambers are in use, the members are not lined up facing each other as if prepared for war, like the armies in First World War trenches. There are several theories of design that promise to deliver calm deliberation rather than conflict; perhaps the parliamentary architects could study the subject.

Another important modification would be to introduce a modern system of proportional representation to the House of Representatives to reverse the trend toward oligarchy. The diversity of representation achieved by such a reform would almost certainly lead to more political parties in the House, because smaller parties would have a greater chance of gaining election. To achieve this within the Constitution, the states could be divided into electorates with five, six or seven seats. However, it would only happen if there were dramatic changes of attitude in the major parties or if they were to lose their joint domination of the House.

Cooperative Government

The exciting prospect of a constitutional change of the electoral system is explored in Chapter 11, 'Does Australia's Representative Democracy Represent Us'. The form of parliament envisaged there is uni-cameral and multi-party, with equal numbers of men and women. It would legislate on tasks that require national regulation or coordination, leaving local and regional issues to be resolved at an appropriate level. What sort of executive government would such a parliament create? The current form of majority government would be improbable, because a dominant one-party majority would be unlikely. Coalition (small 'c') governments are one possibility, but perhaps the most productive and stable form would be a cooperative government, similar to that functioning successfully in Switzerland[5].

Based on the Swiss experience, Australia could be run by a ten-minister cooperative government that would include all the significant parties. Elected under proportional representation by a representative parliament, ten people would be enough to form a government, because they would not need to waste their time trying to outwit the other side or repealing the measures introduced by a previous government. Moreover, a ministry of that size would be involved only with the important issues at a national level. Under a cooperative government, issues are more likely to be resolved in the national interest than in accord with party policies or the demands of financial supporters. Such an arrangement would be unfamiliar, if not unbelievable to most Australians. It would require a transformation in the behaviour of many practicing politicians or the induction of cooperative politicians who behave differently. However, the record of politicians who have retired from politics suggest that it is the system, rather than the inherent qualities of the participants, that give rise to the adversarial excesses that are so familiar in Australian politics.

Provision could also be made for electing a number of ministers with particular abilities from outside the parliament. There are almost certainly competent potential ministers that cannot be bothered with the turmoil of campaigning for a seat in parliament, which is a loss to the country.

The executive government elected by the parliament would be the virtual 'head-of-state' and parliament itself would comprise the government's 'opposition' while creating and maintaining standing committees to monitor the government's performance and to unearth expert advice on matters relevant to decision-making. Parliamentary standing committees could also undertake tasks such as recruitment for government services, defining and auditing financial standards, investigating the claims of 'whistleblowers', etc. The 'reserve powers' of the Governor-General would be abolished with the office.

The powers of the parliament would be limited to legislating for those tasks that require national regulation or coordination; local government would do the rest, acting collaboratively when necessary. The ability of local governments to collaborate in undertaking tasks and functions for the mutual interests in their region should not be doubted; the Melbourne and Metropolitan Board of Works is an example of this; established in the nineteenth century, it became a world leader in water supply and sewerage management. The experience of the author working in small rural communities is that, when required to meet a challenge, amazing people 'pop out of the woodwork'. Chapter 5, on 'Local Sector Reform', describes other contemporary organizations, while new examples are being reported from time to time.

Government structures in the form of existing functional regions would allow local government to assume a monitoring or supervisory role in sub-national government functions with minimal disruption. These regions are described in Chapter 8, 'Governing without State Governments'. It can be seen that no new government entities would be required to effect a dramatic and beneficial change to the governance of Australia, a change to a lower cost model that would also be more responsive to the constituent communities of Australia. This model is described and evaluated in Chapter 12.

In effect, the result would be in accord with the principles of subsidiarity; that is to say, the national government would only perform those tasks that are beyond the scope of local governments, the tier of government closest to the people.

Endnotes

1 Marchant Leslie R, 1999, "The Westminster Tradition and Australia", Hesperian Press, page 14.

2 Fraser, Malcolm, with Roberts, Cain, 2014, "Dangerous Allies", Melbourne University Press.

3 Marchant, ibid, page 64.

4 Actually, they are very well paid and enjoy exclusive privileges, not as experts but as community representatives.

5 Switzerland has only 0.5% the area of Australia, ¼ the population and four official languages; those differences would be relevant in a discussion on gardening, but not one on governance.

Chapter 14

The Constitution and the Indigenous people

Klaas Woldring

Preface: The Indigenous Recognition Panel

Executive summary (2011)

Current multiparty support has created a historic opportunity to recognise Aboriginal and Torres Strait Islander peoples as the first peoples of Australia, to affirm their full and equal citizenship, and to remove the last vestiges of racial discrimination from the Constitution.

The Expert Panel was tasked to report to the Government on possible options for constitutional change to give effect to indigenous constitutional recognition, including advice as to the level of support from indigenous people and the broader community for these options. It made the following recommendations:

1. That section 25 be repealed.

2. That section 51(xxvi) be repealed.

3. That a new 'section 51A' be inserted, along the following lines: Section 51A Recognition of Aboriginal and Torres Strait Islander peoples Recognising that the continent and its islands now known as Australia were first occupied by Aboriginal and Torres Strait Islander peoples; Acknowledging the continuing relationship of Aboriginal and Torres Strait Islander peoples with their traditional lands and waters; Respecting the continuing cultures, languages and heritage of Aboriginal and Torres Strait Islander peoples; Acknowledging the need to secure the advancement of Aboriginal and Torres Strait Islander peoples; the Parliament shall,

subject to this Constitution, have power to make laws for the peace, order and good government of the Commonwealth with respect to Aboriginal and Torres Strait Islander peoples. The Panel further recommends that the repeal of section 51(xxvi) and the insertion of the new 'section 51A' be proposed together.

4.   That a new 'section 116A' be inserted, along the following lines: Section 116A Prohibition of racial discrimination

   (1) The Commonwealth, a State or a Territory shall not discriminate on the grounds of race, colour or ethnic or national origin.

   (2) Subsection (1) does not preclude the making of laws or measures for the purpose of overcoming disadvantage, ameliorating the effects of past discrimination, or protecting the cultures, languages or heritage of any group.

5.   5 That a new 'section 127A' be inserted, along the following lines: Section 127A Recognition of languages

   (1) The national language of the Commonwealth of Australia is English.

   (2) The Aboriginal and Torres Strait Islander languages are the original Australian languages, a part of our national heritage.

The Gillard Government first decided (in 2010) that a referendum should be held on these recommendations or at least on some of them. Later it withdrew that proposal. The referendum to acknowledge Indigenous Australians was shelved for at least three years amid fears of failure to build community support before the deadline of the next election would see it defeated.

The Gillard Government instead asked Parliament to pass an "Act of Recognition" to acknowledge "the unique and special place of our first peoples" as an "interim" measure until there is enough support for a constitutional change.

Julia Gillard talked to Tony Abbott and the Greens about Labor's intention to introduce the symbolic act in a formal admission that a referendum would fail if it were put to a vote in 2013 as planned. As part of Labor's 2010 power-sharing agreement with the Greens and Independents, Labor had agreed to hold a referendum on Indigenous constitutional recognition before or at the 2013 election.

Indigenous Affairs Minister Jenny Macklin said a sunset clause on the proposed act would force the Parliament not to neglect the issue. "We have a sunset clause in the bill of say two or three years so that the next parliament really has to look at it and make sure that we maintain the community awareness and continue to have a discussion for the need for constitutional change, not just in the area of recognition but on the other matters the expert panel raised," she said.

In February, 2013 the Act of Recognition was passed with bi-partisan support. Julia Gillard and Tony Abbott committed themselves to address what Ms. Gillard called "the unhealed wound that even now lies open at the heart of our national story" and the Opposition Leader dubbed "this stain on our soul".

However, Abbott as PM has hosed down calls made during 2014 to recognise Indigenous Australians in the Constitution during the current parliamentary term, saying "the landmark reform needs to put to the people when it is most likely to succeed."

The Garma Festival in Arnhem land – the ABC's Q and A program.

At the Garma Festival (4th August, 2014) the issue was tackled head on during the unique ABC program broadcast from there. The very first question focused on the desirability or otherwise to try to rectify the current Constitution, a set of rules from which the Indigenous people were entirely excluded, and are still largely excluded. As is demonstrated in this text it is also in need of a complete rewrite for a large number of other reasons. Indigenous recognition in this archaic Constitution would be a special instance of piecemeal tinkering. While long overdue and desirable, again Government was most apprehensive that such a referendum would fail. Instead an Act of Recognition was passed, a kind of consolation measure.

The position taken here is that the rewriting of the Constitution must take place with the total inclusion of ALL Australian citizens. That automatically includes the Indigenous people. In that sense a new Constitution represents a Treaty between all the citizens.

What follows now is part of an abstract of the first session of that ABC program that covered about 12 minutes.

Abstract of the views on Indigenous recognition in the current Constitution (part of transcript provided by the ABC)

TONY JONES: Good evening and welcome to Q&A. I'm Tony Jones. Please thank our four yidaki players, led by Djalu Gurruwiwi, representing the four directions of this land for that wonderful welcome. Now, we - okay, yes, we can clap as well. We begin tonight's Q&A by acknowledging the traditional owners of this land.

We're in Yolngu country in the remote north east corner of Arnhem land as guests of the Yothu Yindi Foundation and the Garma Festival and answering your questions tonight: the CEO of the Northern Land Council Joe Morrison; Australia's most influential Indigenous leader Noel Pearson; Gälpu Clan Elder and businesswoman Dhäŋggal Gurruwiwi; the deputy of the Yothu Yindi Foundation, Djawa Yunupingu ; Olympic gold, Labor Senator for the Northern Territory Nova Peris; and the first Aboriginal elected to the House of Representatives, Liberal MP Ken Wyatt. Please welcome our panel.

Thank you. Now, Q&A is simulcast on ABC News 24 and News Radio. you can join the Twitter conversation using the #qanda hashtag on your screen as usual. Now, this is a night of firsts. The first Q&A focused on Australia's first people and the first Q&A to include so many Indigenous people on the panel and in the audience. So let's get straight to our first question, which comes from Jazlie Grugoruk.

Re: Constitutional Recognition

JAZLIE GRUGORUK: Thanks, Tony. My question's for the whole panel. The Australian constitution and the Australian state were founded on the myth of terra nullius: the assertion that Australia was uninhabited at the time of settlement. As an Indigenous person who has lost my language, my culture and identity under white colonialism, why should I assent to falsely established Australian law by asking to include my people within its founding document? A treaty is the only way to assert our original sovereignty and equality, so why are you, with respect, our Indigenous leaders, settling for a watered down attempt at recognition in the Australian Constitution?

TONY JONES: Well, Ken Wyatt, we'll start with you because you are the chair of the parliamentary committee into the constitutional referendum on recognition, so let's hear what you say to this idea it should be a treaty?

KEN WYATT: Tony, I think it's great that we have the questioning occurring because part of the process is for all of us to have the dialogue but what we've got to remember is Australia was only known as Australia from 1788. Before that it had several other names. But Aboriginal and Torres Strait Islander people have had a continuity of existence with this land for that period of time. They were left out of the constitutional conventions. They were left out of the 1901. We live in this country and we deserve to be recognised within the constitution but that doesn't negate aspirations for those who want treaty or sovereignty. When Australia is ready for that, that debate can occur in the future.

TONY JONES: So two things are possible?

KEN WYATT: Two things are possible.

TONY JONES: Nova Peris?

NOVA PERIS: For me this whole discussion, you know, it's - like what you're saying, you know, there's a lot of Aboriginal people that have lost their identities since colonisation and the significance of being recognised in this document is, to me and to other Aboriginal people, it's about the true history of this country, the entire genetic makeup of this country, what is now called Australia, and it would be wrong to say that you would continue to lose more by having this important, I guess, conversation is what we're having now with the Australia public and, you know, there's so many Australians, you know, through the terra nullius, through land rights, through there's so many historical things that have occurred but this is so important on an international level and also to Aboriginal people because we will finally be seen as citizens that make up this country.

TONY JONES: Nova, do you worry that the broader Australian public hasn't yet focussed on this, don't really understand what it's all about?

NOVA PERIS: Well, that is true and I think, you know, we need to acknowledge the recognised movement who have actually gotten out there and they've made a tremendous contribution to having that discussion amongst the wider community. We see at the AFL, you know, there are a number of national sporting organisations that are onboard this and we need to have the conversations. You know, we're talking about human beings being inclusive in a country, you know, what we call Australia and, as we all know, we're the oldest collective race in the world and I say this every time I have conversations, Australia doesn't lose 230 years, you gain 40,000 years of history.

TONY JONES: How do you answer directly the young woman's question? She's asking why a constitutional referendum for a constitution that doesn't mean anything to her as, as she puts it, what's necessary in her mind is a treaty.

NOVA PERIS: I guess that's a conversation that a lot of individuals would be thinking. You know, when you talk about treaties, when you talk about, you know, how far we've come now as Australians, there's a debate to be had with regards to what could possibly go to the Australian public and we can't lose that momentum. You know, we've got to continue on because it's, as Aboriginal people we are excluded, you know. For such a long time we were regarded as flora and fauna you know and it's about making a wrong right.

TONY JONES: Noel Pearson?

NOEL PEARSON: Tony, I was 24 years old when I went to one of the most galvanising seminars, where I heard Michael Mansell speak for the first time on the subject of a treaty between the Aboriginal sovereign nation and the Australian nation. I was just a law student at the time and it was a real challenge that Mansell raised at the end of that seminar and his question at the end of it was are we Australian Aborigines or Aboriginal Australians and he challenged us that we need to make a choice, one way or the other, and I suppose in all of my advocacy I am making the case that we are Aboriginal Australians, that the nation of Australia can carve out a recognition and a space for our people as a distinct people and with distinct traditions. I would say to the young lady that I don't accept that she's lost her identity. I come across tens of thousands of Aboriginal people who live in a great variety of different circumstances and I see their traditions. I see their heritage and I see their entitlement for recognition and, of course, there's a big spectrum. I come here to Arnhem Land really to share a part of the classical culture, which used to exist all over the continent on the four corners and but that doesn't deny, in my view, the fact that if you're living in Sydney, if you're living in Melbourne, if you're living on the eastern seaboard, that you don't have an identity. You know, I think it's desperately important that we reach a settlement with the rest of Australia about protecting and, for the first time, recognising that identity.

TONY JONES: Noel, what do you think should be in the referendum question because we heard Bill Shorten here yesterday say there needs to be written into the constitution as the expert panel on this suggested actually, a protection against discrimination?

NOEL PEARSON: Well, it's discrimination that's kind of underwritten our parlous position in this country. It's been the source of the great miseries that we have ensured. It was discrimination that left us out of the constitution in the first place. I think the question that we will go through as we discuss the expert panel's report and the report produced by the committee that Nova and Ken were members of is the question of whether some kind of guarantee against discrimination is part of the provisions that are taken forward or whether Aboriginal people need to have a say over their own affairs so that, you know, we decide that we - what applies to our people and the protections and recognition that we deserve and I think this is a big question. It'll play out over the next two years probably and I look forward to a good debate about this.

TONY JONES: Djawa, the great Yothu Yindi song everyone remembers, I'm sure, is Treaty and the chorus went, "Treaty now." What do you think? Do you think it's time for a treaty or constitutional referendum or can you have both?

DJAWA YUNUPINGU: When my brother wrote the song about treaty, it was only a song. The song was written because the former Prime Minister when he said "There shall be a treaty" and that was back in 1998, right?

TONY JONES: Long time ago.

TONY JONES: But you would encourage people to go out and vote in the referendum and be part of the big debate about the referendum as well when it happens?

DHÄNGGAL GURRUWIWI: I would.

TONY JONES: Joe Morrison?

JOE MORRISON: I think the question about constitutional recognition represents an enormous step forward in the maturing of the country and we've seen, for a long time, many important events that have galvanised Aboriginal people. You know, the pastoral awards, strike in the Pilbara, land rights, Mabo, things here in the Northern Territory, like the Barunga Statement, have been profoundly important events that have galvanised people and I think the question of the constitutional recognition shouldn't be seen as being exclusive to all other attempts to bring the country into a high level of maturity and I think that's in the context that it should be taken that this is a profoundly important step for the nation to make. It's a profoundly important step for Aboriginal people to embrace the country and for the rest of the country to embrace the uniqueness that Aboriginal people bring so I think it is something that is worthwhile pursuing. It's worthwhile pursuing for my own kids, as well was their kids, to be able to enjoy the fruits of the country and all that it brings and I would wholeheartedly recommend that we pursue it but not take our eye off other opportunities in the future.

TONY JONES: Okay, let's move on.

KEN WYATT: Tony, just on that.

TONY JONES: Yes, go on, Ken. Yes, go ahead.

KEN WYATT: Can I say to the young lady the 1967 referendum changed the mindset of Australians towards our people. The speech by Paul Keating at Redfern was a landmark speech of recognition of the challenges of the past and the dispossession that occurred and then the apology healed so many of us, including my mother, who was from the stolen generation, and the next step was then to move to the completion of the constitution and from that we will build to the stages that will complete the social fabric of this nation to make it a nation in which we are all equals.

TONY JONES: Ken, just very briefly - we've got lots of other questions to go to - but do you think you could potentially see a treaty in your lifetime?

KEN WYATT: Probably not in my lifetime. I'm much older now than what I used to be in the period that Noel was talking about but I think Australia, in its grown and maturation will reach a point where there will be arrangements that go into place and treaty is a word that certainly a Prime Minister committed to but never followed up with.

Chapter 15

Planning to achieve a truly democratic 21st century Australian Constitution

Geoff Armstrong

1. 1788 - Democracy denied

It is frequently claimed the 1901 Constitution has served us well for more than a century, but those who make the claim clearly have little understanding of what 'democracy' means, or much appreciation of the skill and care required to ensure a soundly based national constitution will remain relevant in an evolving world.

'Failing to plan is planning to fail' is a cliché quoted by professional planners. In Australia's case bad planning, manipulated planning, or sometimes no planning at all, have repeatedly made such failures inevitable. Australia has been subjected to them since it was first selected in the mid-1780s as a dumping ground for surplus British convicts. It began with poor planning advice from botanist Joseph Banks, who accompanied explorer/navigator Cook on his 1770s voyage to the Pacific, and said when they returned to England that Botany Bay was fertile enough to rapidly make such a colony self-sufficient (both soil and timber later proved to be unsuitable), and there were not enough natives present to provide serious opposition to settlement (they were numerous, but most were hiding in or watching from the bush). When, in January 1788, 'the first fleet' of eleven boats with almost 1500 on board (including 778 convicts) arrived to establish the initial colony, it had a leader (Governor Phillip) who was a fine sailor and navigator, but who knew nothing about farming. It brought few builders, farmers or gardeners amongst the convicts; a poorly chosen supply of tools; and it had an unpredictable climate to deal with. Famine soon forced any thought of self-sufficiency to be abandoned.

The new settlement was intended to be, as cynics in London nicknamed it, *'a colony of* "thieves"', and was never planned or expected to become a nation. Convicts who had hoped to return to Britain once their sentences had expired soon found that remoteness and cost made this impossible. Although Phillip's first edict (he said there was to be no slavery in a free land) was promising, few of the released convicts could find legitimate or gainful employment other than as virtual slaves of members of the 'upper classes.'

There was no hint of democracy for them. The colony was managed in that vein until the mid-nineteenth century even though there was a steady change in the free settler/convict balance with the arrival of increasing numbers of paying emigrants, many of whom were anti-British poor evicted from Scotland and Ireland, and gold-rush immigrants from other countries.

In 1853 the British government passed the Australian Colonies Government Act to counter the enthusiasm for creation of a republic that had been developing in NSW, and hoping to see '...*the growth of democracy in Australia checked by stable institutions...*' Each colony, commencing with NSW, was invited to prepare its own constitution and become an individual state. The acceptance of this offer by each colony in turn virtually ensured that, when an Australian constitution came under debate later in the nineteenth century, a divisive structure of a federation and six states with individual constitutions and competing goals would be unavoidable.

2. 1901 - Democracy deferred

The drafting of an Australian constitution was placed in the hands of a panel of conservative representatives elected or appointed by the six states. Were these 19th century politicians competent to produce a national constitution capable of dealing with the inevitable challenges of the 20th century? Although their understanding of words like 'constitution' and 'democracy' might have seemed appropriate to meet 19th century challenges, is it realistic to argue that they are still capable of doing so today? There was even debate between the members of the 1890s panel about whether the common people should be consulted or their views considered. When the final draft was adopted in 1901 as the Australian Constitution, it concluded with a clause (s. 128) which would make amendment of their masterpiece by commoners virtually impossible without the prior consent and action of politicians. So much for 'democracy'! Their draft constitution was rejected by the first referendum in 1891, but was passed by the second in 1899, not because it was made more democratic, but because changes acceptable to the states were made to strengthen political and state dominance. It has remained virtually unchanged since.

This should not necessarily be seen as an indictment of those who drafted the 1901 Constitution, but more a criticism of those still defending its value now. In 1882 (immediately before the drafting of the 1901 constitution), a revised edition of the then widely used Chambers Dictionary was printed, in which its definition of 'constitution' was '...a system of laws and customs; the established form of government' ...and it becomes understandable why the 1890s panel supported the adoption of both the established Westminster model of government, and retention of the British monarchy in an ongoing role in Australian politics. They were both essential to the panel's understanding of an 'established form of government'. The Shorter Oxford Dictionary 1967 became a little more helpful to today's planners by defining 'constitution' as 'the system or body of fundamental principles according to which a nation, state, or body politic is constituted and governed', but that concept still relies too heavily on the past to provide a guide to the future. That was the mistake made when the 1890s panel was chosen and given its instructions.

As now High Chief Court Justice French wrote in 'Reflections on the Constitution' (2008): 'Those who voted on the original constitutional Bill in 1890/91 were defined by a limited franchise... women and Aborigines were excluded...'

More appropriate and contemporary advice about constitution drafting is set out in a recent work by Google Ideas, which states 'Constitutions are as unique as the people they govern...The process of redesigning and drafting a new constitution can play a critical role in uniting a country, especially following *periods of conflict and instability...Our aim is to arm drafters with a better tool for constitution design and writing.'* Google's assistance has come at a time when Australia has been experiencing considerable political conflict and instability, and we sorely need a catalyst to unite the nation. But it is not Beyond Federation's job to seek or accept that role. To determine who should do so first requires further careful review of the word *'democracy',* a word that is bandied about by politicians world–wide without any evidence that many of them understand, respect or support its true value.

'Democracy' is recognised in all dictionaries consulted as having been derived from the ancient Greek words for 'people (demos), and 'rule', to mean (SOD) *'...that form of government in which the sovereign power resides in the people, and is exercised either by them or by officers elected by them...'* and it adds *'...that class of the people which has no hereditary rank or distinction...'* The carefully chosen words *'elected by them...'* and *'...no hereditary rank or distinction'* immediately bring into focus just one of the many reasons why the 1901 Constitution has to be completely revised, and not merely amended or rewritten to make it truly democratic.

Finally, having defined *'constitution'* and *'democracy'* in acceptable terms, it is next vital that the word *'planning'* and its responsibilities are even more carefully understood, because they will become the lynch-pin necessary to initiate the democratic planning process and determine the steps we must follow to achieve our goal.

A basic definition of *'Planning'* is provided in the 1967 edition of the Shorter Oxford Dictionary as *'...a scheme of action, the way in which it is proposed to carry out some proceeding...',* but this definition is too simplistic and restrictive to provide the guidance now needed to review our national constitution, which is more than 'some proceeding'. It has to be better qualified, more comprehensive, and, unlike the 1901 model it must encourage lateral, constructive thinking. A national constitution must be a plan for the future, not a reincarnation of the past.

A more suitable concept would be that practised by the author of this chapter when planning the management of natural areas (State Forests, National Parks, and other conservation areas). It was based on three p's –

philosophy, principle, and process. In writing our national Constitution these guidelines should be presented in a preamble (the underlying ***philosophy***); in the specific statements and directions in the body of the plan necessary to guide the politicians governing the country and to set out the rights and responsibilities of its citizens throughout the life of the plan (the ***principles***); and in an action plan on how to do the job *(the **process***). A good example of what a new Australian Constitution should contain is provided by the widely respected Australian jurist Geoffrey Robertson in his recent book: '*Dreaming Out Loud*', in which he provides a draft '*Preamble*', and a '*Charter of Australian Liberty*' written for contemporary and likely future Australian conditions.

But who should complete the preparation of the plan designed to ensure democracy in Australia from the 21st century on? How can this be done successfully, when others have not succeeded in the 113 years since adoption of the Constitution in 1901?

Beyond Federation, in spite of its small number of members, limited finance, and absence of business organization, has already been bold enough to initiate and promote the urgent need to review the 1901 Constitution, and to develop a process capable of ensuring that genuinely democratic government will result. But it must not become it's responsibility to complete the task.

A London clergyman once wrote on his public notice board: '*Apathy is the curse of our generation!*' below which a reply was promptly written: '*Who cares?*' Many of our citizens might also say: '*Who Cares?*' But we must all care if we are to help make up the numbers essential to attain our goal – a genuinely democratic 21st century Constitution 'as unique as the people it governs'; a 21st century Australian Constitution. How can this be legally achieved? What steps must we take to ensure it is both democratically written, and capable of passing the s.128 challenge, which was seemingly written by its politically motivated authors to make any amendment virtually impossible without adequate majority party/political support? At present, to win Constitutional amendment any referendum proposed must first be approved by an absolute majority in each House of Parliament;

then by a majority of electors in a majority of states; and finally (third in the pecking order) by a majority of electors throughout the nation.

Past attempts by sincere lobby groups to obtain constitutional amendment have consistently failed for reasons other than those they could simplistically attribute to s.128. Most common has been the 'go it alone' approach they regularly adopt, copying the traditional trade union street march routine of demanding what they want and when they want it, independently of, and sometimes in conflict with, other groups seeking different but equally justifiable changes. For more than a century now, such groups insistent on 'going it alone', have been effectively dividing the ranks of progressive constitution critics seeking change, and at the same time giving opponents (who frequently include the government) reasons and ammunition with which to respond.

Further such failures will only be avoided if lobby groups abandon their unwinnable 'go it alone' approach and persuade compatible groups to unite (if only pro tem) into one large lobby group with one common goal; that of achieving bipartisan agreement to democratically review and replace the 1901 Constitution. Provided competition between individual lobby groups is honestly and cooperatively put on hold until after adequate political support for the major goal has been committed and the review is in progress, this policy should provide adequate numbers to persuade all politicians sensitive to poll trends to give their support.

3. 2014/2016 - Democracy at Last?

By preparing this eBook, *Beyond Federation* has taken the essential step in promoting the campaign to have the Australian Constitution democratically reviewed and replaced. It has long been acknowledged that too many Australians are ignorant of or disinterested in their nation's Constitution, and Beyond Federation's initiative will surely assist in overcoming this problem.

But knowledge alone is not going to solve Australia's constitutional dilemma. It certainly is a prerequisite, but even when it has been present in many past contributions it has failed to make much impact on the status quo. This will only be achieved as stated throughout this chapter by sound planning. The whole process should, as Google forecast, be designed to unite the nation. The process should proceed as follows:

Step 1: To develop sufficient clout to persuade politicians to accede to our democratic proposals, Beyond Federation must immediately seek more supporters, initially through negotiation with already committed lobby groups. We must ensure the motives and principles of those invited or who volunteer to join us will not clash with those of other participants. To achieve this delicate but vital balance it is suggested potential supporters be asked to commit to: (i) join Beyond Federation pro tem in creating one combined lobby group with one united goal - that of seeking political support to comprehensively overhaul the Australian Constitution; (ii) put their own individual goals on hold until adequate political agreement to a democratic review of the 1901 Constitution has been promised; (iii) work with other supporters cooperatively until sufficient political support for (i) above has been committed.

Once political support has been promised, the individual groups could then resume their former programs and strategies, although hopefully the cooperative atmosphere created might reduce the antagonism of any past encounters.

While the above steps are proceeding, discussions should be continuing on the case to be presented to politicians on how the writing of a new constitution must proceed. It has been previously argued within Beyond Federation the review must be conducted by a democratically chosen (invited, elected, or appointed) panel; funded by the government; and instructed to involve frequent communication and debate with the community on its direction and progress. Panel hearings must be publicly conducted.

Nationally Australia would be the winner as action to produce a new Constitution could then proceed in an atmosphere of cooperation in lieu of the divisiveness regularly seen in the past. Refusal to join the combined lobby group pro tem should be very much to an offending group's disadvantage when competition is resumed, as it could well be seen as having put its own individual goals above those of the nation.

Step 2: Bring the media on board a.s.a.p. The eBook should receive recognition, promotion at public meetings and in the media, and for the first time the media would have a united and common and comprehensive cause to debate and hopefully support.

Step 3: Initiate negotiations with all political parties and politicians when the political climate is favourable, and when media interest has been fully aroused. Desirably, this would be when the fortunes of the major parties are no longer tied to the adversarial two-party system, and multi-partisan agreements are needed to achieve majorities.

Failure by any party or politician to cooperate with the planning and implementation of the constitutional overhaul may well be appropriately punished via the ballot box at the first subsequent election.

In summary, the constitutional review must be conducted with multi-partisan agreement and parliamentary approval, and insistence by all that Australia-wide democratic input and citizen involvement throughout will be essential. The draft constitution must be prepared by a carefully chosen apolitical drafting panel, with an independent and prestigious Chairperson (e,g., a former GG, High Court member...), which should be directed to conduct public meetings and hearings to consider each case presented for inclusion in the final draft of the new Constitution.

The final act will be for the draft to be presented, as required under s.128 of the current Constitution, for approval by referendum.

Conclusion

The principal messages of the book speak for themselves. Although many would say that such major changes as have been suggested in this text would be very difficult to achieve, here is a set of arguments that present real alternatives. These ideas are indeed all forward-looking. They reject further piecemeal tinkering and deny that the existing Constitution is a living, democratic document. They also reject other related realities, e.g. the notion that federation still has anything useful to offer; and e.g., as Anthony Nicholas demonstrates, that our electoral systems achieve fair and democratic representation of the society in our parliaments.

This latter point is very relevant indeed because Australia has been struggling with a dominant two-party system in which the one party can best be described as a mostly conservative Labor Party and the other as a reactionary conservative party. The mildly redeeming factors in this adversarial system are a more diverse Senate, although elected by an outmoded and perverted variety of proportional representation, and a judiciary that has generally enjoyed respect of the population. The Senate has on occasions formed a barrier to radical conservatism, as could be claimed again in 2014, but on other occasions it has also been a barrier to progressive reform. In relation to constitutional reform, most expert commentators are firmly of the view that the limits of meaningful interpretation by judges was reached long ago in most areas.

However, what has happened since the September 2013 federal election is in many ways a trend that is the exact opposite of what has been recommended by the contributors in this book. In many policy areas the Abbott government has been inspired and supported by free marketeers who believe that the Government sector should be as small as possible, competition is a desirable way to achieve public good, and individual freedoms, such as freedom of expression, should be given full rein. A first Budget was presented that has experienced great difficulty to be approved in the Senate and was widely seen as unfair. The underlying motivation was claimed to be a Budget crisis caused by the previous ALP Government in spite of the fact that most economists and financial commentators demonstrated that there is no major crisis at all. While these policy and budget issues are outside the scope of this book, the attitude of the Abbott government towards federation certainly is part of it. Completely contrary to Abbott's views expressed at a federalism conference of 2008, his Government has adopted competitive federalism ideology, further evidence that it is trying to turn the clock back also in this area. In a similar fashion as its attitude towards public broadcasters, it is of the view that private sector strategies of competition should be applied to public sector institutions and management styles. In the realm of federal government this has resulted in the notion that tax powers should be returned to the states, an idea that originated apparently with the Commission of Audit. Such a backward step would then result in the states becoming fully engaged in competition among themselves and that, presumably, would achieve superior outcomes at lower cost.

Several commentators have pointed out that tax dodgers would love such a development but this is only one aspect of the negative consequences. As Mark Drummond has shown in his PhD thesis (2007) and in earlier collaborations with Jim Snow (1995) and Rodney Hall (1998), as summarised in this text (see Chapter 4), the cost of federation is already an enormous and unnecessary burden on Australia. We should move away from this altogether if we are to achieve real savings. For Australia to have one set of laws and one-taxation system would benefit us all. If we are to further illustrate the current problems of federalism we only have to refer to the election funding corruption that has been revealed by the NSW Independent Commission Against Corruption in recent years. In particular, during 2014 ICAC revealed that several state Liberal MPs were funded for the 2011 state election via donations to two sham bodies, one of which was the Liberal Party's federal front organization known as The Free Enterprise Foundation. Donations from developers, which were outlawed in NSW in 2010, could be channeled via the Canberra-based Foundation to the NSW candidates, thereby subverting the state legislation. One could argue that this "ingenious" scheme is not illegal, even though it corrupts the NSW system, but it would not happen if we had uniform legislation. Hence the calls for another ICAC at the federal level! Could we end up with seven ICACs?

Apart from the overriding problems associated with the federal system, three areas of constitutional inadequacy are very obvious: the total lack of mention in the Constitution of the need to protect the environment, the lack of recognition of the Indigenous people as equal citizens, and the failure to spell out the role of the Parliament or the people in decisions to involve Australia in wars. Environmental values and the need to combat climate change are of such importance now that it is unthinkable that these global priorities are not dealt with in a Constitution. These issues can no longer be subject to the whims or short-term interests of political parties. There have to be firm ground rules for the nation that ensure sufficient continuity of commitment and purpose. As to the position of the Indigenous people and the related issue of racism, surely this cannot be left to ordinary legislation anymore. Furthermore, the current cautious preparedness to recognize the Indigenous people in the Constitution (in 2017!) appears to be such a difficult change to achieve, given the several current constitutional and political system hurdles, that an entirely new Constitution for all Australians clearly makes a lot more sense. As to the decision power to engage Australia in war, recent events have again brought this issue to the fore. What appears to be "normal" to the current P. M. and several others before him, is neither desirable nor democratic at all. Even in the UK, conservative P. M. David Cameron does not want to involve the UK in renewed combat in Iraq without Parliamentary approval. That Westminster practice appears not to apply to Australia. What rules this decision, essentially limited to the Australian P.M. and advice to him by the military, is a request from the US President. There need not even be parliamentary debate, let alone a vote, referendum or plebiscite.

The difficulties of initiating major governance and electoral system changes are many and the received wisdom is that a major crisis is required before the people become seriously motivated to find out what should be done. This period may well have arrived. Cracks in the system are appearing but attempts to put the clock back would seem to us the wrong remedy. The current *Reform of the Federation White Paper*, which is being developed to produce a Green Paper in 2015, is a case in point. It still talks about "renewing federation" and "reforming federation", making sure "our federation is working". It is being developed by a Federalism Taskforce within the Department of the Prime Minister and Cabinet. What this means is that there will be further piecemeal tinkering, the very approach rejected in this text. Of course, one could hardly expect anything else from an ultra conservative Government. Sadly however, few other remedies are being discussed by the Australian intelligentsia, in the universities and by the major media. However, the people have started to protest on a wide front. The popular movements GetUp and MarchAustralia, together with an outpouring on social media, are indicative of a new awakening in Australia. As to Governance issues, the Australian Constitutional Values Survey, October 2014, done by Professor AJ Brown of Griffith University's Centre for Governance and Public Policy, found the following: total respondents with negative view of the present system, in practice or principle during 2008, 2010, 2014 was 86%, 90%, 89% and 84% respectively. To us it seems that the time for piecemeal tinkering is well and truly past. Our primary aim here is to contribute to major renewal options in the governance and political spheres. We will send the Federalism Taskforce a copy of our book.

Appendix I

New Federation – Same Problem

Comment on the late Richard Murray's Paper

Anthony Nicholas

The Australian Financial Review of 14 September 2012 published, on p37, a story on a proposal by Richard Murray to modify the Constitution. His experience in the upper echelons of the public service and as a Board Director at the International Monetary Fund has given him an unusual vantage point. The Australian and New Zealand School of Government published his paper, which contains considerable detail on the dysfunction of Australia's constitutional arrangements. But, it also provides convincing evidence that governance in Australia must advance *beyond federation.*

We Australians have three tiers of government, Commonwealth, state and local. Yet, our existing Constitution is a two-tier model comprising only the Commonwealth and the States. Nevertheless, Murray proposes to leave local government out of the Constitution, where it is neither included nor implied. The proposition to recognise local government in the Australian Constitution has been defeated in two referendums and a recent review by an expert panel did not encourage a third attempt.

Murray proposes a second tier of 'cities and regions' to replace the states and their five hundred and sixty four local governments and illustrates it in a map in which the original states are divided into twenty four parts with a felt-tipped pen, allowing some adjustment at state borders. In dictionaries, a region is described as, *"A part of the earth's surface with a definable characteristic, with or without fixed boundaries".* The 'regions' of Murray's model should be called 'mini-states' or 'territories', because for the most part they do not have definable, identifying qualities. They would be sub-national governments. Surprisingly, they include local governments, despite their omission from the constitution. Moreover, the fixed regional boundaries of sub-national governments will always be an impediment to governance, introducing unnecessary complication in the provision of services such as water supply and catchment management, as his chapters on micro economic reform attest. The description of the relationships between and within proposed sub-national governments predicts a potential paralysis that would be at least as dysfunctional as those between states and Commonwealth now.

Functional Administrative Regions

Another aspect of community and regional life that must be invisible from the top of the pillars of government are the functional administrative regions that undertake many essential services in both city and country. These are described in the the section on 'Functional Regions' in Chapter 8. They are working now, each within a region specific to its function and could be supervised by boards drawn from local and Commonwealth governments. Local governments already collaborate to provide services such as regional libraries, regional waste management and re-cycling, community health and tourist promotion. Without state governments, other tasks such as public health and education could be managed using the same mechanism.

The Two-Party Oligarchy

Murray ignores a major problem with our constitution in the implied acceptance of the Westminster tradition. Whilst having some invaluable features, which have become the basis of democratic government throughout the world, the Westminster system has also given us a two-party political oligarchy and a dysfunctional, adversarial parliament that wastes the scarce talent available within to form governments. It also allows the prime minister to dominate the parliament, rather than enabling a democratic process whereby the parliament would monitor, supervise or even control the government. His idea that an expanded parliament would provide greater representation is negated by the two-party system arising from the single-member electorates. It would merely allow the election of more incompetent and/or ignorant apparatchiks as representatives of the major parties.

The greatest improvement offered by Murray's proposal is the long overdue assumption of power by the federal government over issues of "national strategic significance", introduced on page 5. However, Murray over-rides that worthy identifying criterion with the inferior procedure of plucking something from a list of 'subjects'. This proposed continuation of a list of subjects and functions, like Section 51 of the 1901 Constitution, would confound the use of a criterion of 'national strategic significance' and leave it isolated.

Surely, the history of the use of the powers of Section 51 would advise against making a new list. To illustrate the futility of list-making, Richard Murray seemed to be unaware of the fact that 'Aviation' is not included in the list of powers allocated to the Commonwealth in Section 51 of the Constitution; the Wright brothers did not fly their airplane until December 1903, nearly three years after Australia's Constitution came into effect on 1 January 1901, a fact that argues strongly against making lists. A referendum in 1937 to include powers over aviation in the Constitution was defeated. In the interim, the Commonwealth assumed this power, but avoided any legal involvement that might unmask its assumption. It is also worth noting that, although the first motorcars were in production from the mid-1880s, the Constitution takes no account of the need for national rules of the road stemming from that development, whereas a blanket allocation to the Commonwealth of power over national issues would have.

Micro-Economic Reform

Murray's concerns about micro-economic reform are discussed around his model for sub-national governments and an underlying concept of the distinction between national and sub-national roles. His most valuable idea, that tasks of 'national strategic significance' should be the province of the national government, remains in the background.

A single blanket power over national issues that allocates all those tasks that require national regulation or coordination to the Commonwealth would be much more effective and understandable than any number of lists of subjects. Such a basic statement in our constitution would create an over-riding rule that our successors could understand and interpret according to the circumstances of their times rather than ours. Preferably, that statement would be in accord with the Principle of Subsidiarity.

But, Murray persists with the idea that a list of subjects is the best way to sort out the proper roles for each tier of government. He does acknowledge that most 'subjects' of government have roles for different tiers. The alternative of setting out powers under major subject headings defies the historical experience that has led to many of our current constitutional difficulties. But, to do both, as in Murray's proposal, would be utterly confusing and lead to contradictions.

Mini-state Governments

Murray's supposition on page 47 that the creation of a 'mini-state' level would

> "...condense State and local government into a single layer, that would sharpen the focus on service delivery of national, urban, regional and local programs, while at the same time opening up opportunities to significantly streamline public administration"

is counter-intuitive and thus unbelievable. His proposed 'mini-states' would require the replacement of some five hundred and sixty local governments by twenty-four mini-states. In the country some are up to 1500 km across, their centres hundreds of kilometres from their people; either local government would have to be rapidly re-invented, or the new 'mini-state' governments would need to be backed up by numerous Indian call-centres. The propensity for these new centralized governments to build bureaucratic empires, together with palaces to accommodate them, would quickly dispose of any savings made by abolishing existing state and local governments.

In summary, Murray's proposal that the national government should be empowered to legislate on matters of 'national strategic significance' is welcome. However, as a Bureaucrats' Constitution, this power is only used to make more lists, most of which would be out-of-date within ten years, a very slight improvement on the Politicians' Constitution we have now. Overall, it is regressive, not only because its emphasis on today's economic problems gives it a short term bias, which is quite unacceptable in a national constitution, but also because it proposes the abolition of local grass-roots democratic processes.

The fact of its publication by ANZSOG has given impetus to the debate on constitutional reform, which is a welcome and valuable development. At some time, our Constitution will evolve **beyond federation** into a workable model of governance; Richard Murray has made a valuable contribution to that process.

Appendix II

Australia United: A Unification Plan for Australia for the Period 2009 to 2020

as at 12 October 2009

I invite the honorable and learned member (Mr. Higgins) to consider this point: If the people of the smaller states are willing to adopt the type of government suggested by our Victorian friends, we can save the expense of ten Houses of Legislature and five Governors, and we can become a truly united people. But we have been sent here to frame a scheme of federation, not of amalgamation.

(Sir Richard Baker of South Australia, speaking at the Third Session of the National Australasian Convention, in Melbourne on 17 March 1898, as recorded on page 2482 of the official report)

The **Australia United** plan comprises objectives, outcomes and a five stage transition plan designed to achieve full Unification for Australia by the year 2020, as follows:

Reform Objectives

- Unification (or amalgamation) of Commonwealth, State and Territory governments to achieve a strong national government
- strengthened local governments

Outcomes

- financial benefits of about $20 billion per annum in the public sector, $40 billion per annum in the private sector, and at least $50 billion (or about five per cent of GDP) across the Australian economy as a whole (in 2009 dollar terms)
- improved democracy and government at national and local levels

- no State or Territory governments
- a seamless national economy
- a seamless national approach to the environment
- a national education system
- a national health system
- a single set of laws for the whole of Australia as part of a national system of law, order and safety
- regional administration and cooperation not constrained by State and Territory borders

Five Stage Transition Plan – to be reviewed on completion of each stage

Stage 1: Foundation Laying (~ 2009 to 2013)

- local government strengthened by constitutional recognition, functional empowerment and increased funding from the Commonwealth government
- abolish State and Territory taxes
- ongoing efforts to establish national health, education and legal systems (such as the efforts to establish the national curriculum, national occupational health and safety laws, and national registration systems for businesses, tradespeople and professionals)
- explain to the public that financial benefits in the order of at least $50 billion per annum in 2009 dollar terms, or about five per cent of GDP, can be achieved across the economy overall under a two-tier government structure comprising national and local governments, but no State and Territory governments

Stage 2: Confirmation (~ 2013)

- referendum calling for the amalgamation of Commonwealth, State and Territory governments to form a single national government under Commonwealth control, leaving local government and regional administration of government functions otherwise unchanged in the first instance

Stage 3: Preparation – After the Referendum at Stage 2 is Carried (~ 2013 to 2016)

- establish a single national set of laws and regulations across all fields, where such laws can host local variations where required for different geographic and climatic conditions (for building regulations, for example), and can be applied at the discretion of local governments, to achieve a seamless national economy and seamless national legal and environmental management systems

- establish fully national funding systems under Commonwealth control for education, health and other functions currently funded at least in part by State and Territory governments

- Commonwealth Grants Commission designs methodologies to provide Commonwealth funding direct to local governments rather than State and Territory governments

Stage 4: Unification Day (2016)

- Commonwealth, State and Territory Governments form a unified national government under Commonwealth control

- Courts previously operating in States and Territories become Commonwealth Courts

- Lands and assets of State and Territory governments are transferred to the Commonwealth

- Unification Transition Bureau is Formed

- State and Territory Parliamentarians have the choice to retire or become part of the Unification Transition Bureau for a maximum of four years

- all employees of State and Territory governments become employees of the Commonwealth government, including education and health sector employees and the police

Stage 5: Consolidation to Achieve Full Unification (2016 to 2020)

- rationalisation of former Commonwealth, State and Territory bureaucracies to achieve a single national government bureaucracy

- generous (all carrot, no stick) incentives and redundancy payout plans for surplus public servants

- transfer of financial and human resources from bureaucracy to local government, schools, hospitals and other "coalface" public service units

- refinement of boundaries used for regional administrative units so they no longer stop at State and Territory borders

- financial benefits amounting to approximately $20 billion per annum in the public sector, $40 billion per annum in the private sector, and at least $50 billion per annum (or about five per cent of GDP) across the economy as a whole, are likely to be achieved from about 2020 onwards after the initial costs of transition more or less cancel out such benefits over the period 2016 to 2019

Dr Mark Drummond
Co-convenor of Beyond Federation (see www.beyondfederation.org.au)
5 Loddon Street Kaleen ACT 2617
phone: 02 6255 0772
email: markld@ozemail.com.au
website: http://members.webone.com.au/~markld/PubPol/GSR/gsr.html

Beyond Federation – backgrounds of contributors

The reader will notice that this is not a typical academic book. The nine contributors represent a great diversity of backgrounds.

Geoff Armstrong

B.Sc. (For.) Dip. For. MIFA. Graduated 1950. 1950-1986; managed (including planning) of natural areas in State Forests and National Parks in NSW. Member on numerous statutory government bodies. Consultant to International Commission CNPPA for 7 years. 1985-1996, developed, managed, then leased ecotourist/environmental study (Wangat Lodge) in Hunter Valley. 1992-5 with wife Isabel transcribed and published 19th century diaries detailing educational, social and political life in NSW. Retired to Canberra 2006.

David Bofinger

David has managed to avoid the political experience and relevant qualifications of some authors in this anthology. His career as a scientist ended after a Ph.D. in theoretical physics, and now he mathematically models naval operations to advise the Australian Department of Defence on what ships the Royal Australian Navy needs to be given. He sees his interest in the reform of federation as an extension of a lifelong love of history, into trying to make it.

Max Bradley

Max is a foundation member of Beyond Federation; has been a Councillor of the rural Berrigan Council, NSW for several years. He developed the "Shed-a-Tier" concept and participated in the thirteen Beyond Federation conferences.

Mark Drummond, Ph. D.

Mark is a founder of Beyond Federation and has been Convener of the Group since 2001. He initiated and organised thirteen Beyond Federation conferences in the eastern States and ACT between 2001 and 2005 and developed the Australia United Plan in 2009. He was in the Australian Navy from 1985 till 1999 and has been a teacher in the Navy, at TAFE, and in universities, and is now a High School mathematics teacher in Canberra.

Anthony Nicholas

Anthony and wife Margaret (who wrote the Preface) is a fourth generation Australian. After dabbling in engineering courses and paid work, he qualified for a BSc (mathematical statistics). Commonwealth Public Service 1959 - 1986, mainly teamwork on quantitative solutions to technical and economic issues. Briefly involved in ALP and, as Policy Coordinator, with the 'Australia Party' until Don Chip's take-over. Part-time lecturing at RMIT in mathematics, statistics & computer programming, before personal computers. "With only one life to live, we moved to a picturesque 140 ha farmlet in 1987, participating in LandCare, a no-toxic-waste campaign, an Ecoliving project; and Aged Care, included establishing the 'Hughes Creek Catchment Collaborative' in 1994, retired from board of Violet Town Bush Nursing Centre in 2011".

Elizabeth Proust A. O.

Ms. Proust delivered the 2013 Kemsley Oration for the Planning Institute Australia, reproduced here with her permission. She has held leadership roles in the private and public sectors in Australia for over 30 years. She has an outstanding track record in leading organisations, and in involvement in a range of arts, charitable, university and business boards, for which she was made an Officer of the Order of Australia in 2010. Elizabeth is Chairman of Nestle Australia Ltd, Chairman of Bank of Melbourne, a director of Perpetual Ltd, Spotless Ltd, Insurance Manufacturers Australia Pty Ltd, Sinclair Knight Merz Holdings Pty Ltd, and of Sports Australia Hall of Fame.

Jim Snow

Jim served as member for Eden Monaro for five terms until 1996 and chaired the Keating government caucus from 1993-1996. Owned and managed pharmacies in Victoria and Canberra. Established Queanbeyan City Council's Community Workers' Department between 1975 and 1977. Raised stud angora goats for 17 years. Qualified at the Victorian College of Pharmacy (now part of Monash University). Voluntary youth probation officer Victoria, President and Secretary of the Salaried Pharmacists Association, Honorary Lieutenant pharmacist, Army Reserve for many years. Former convenor of Beyond Federation, and member of the Drug Law Reform Foundation.

Justin Smith

Justin Smith is a broadcaster, journalist and writer. He has spent his career working in Australian radio. Formerly, he was the executive producer of the Neil Mitchell program at 3AW, Melbourne, as well as presenting his own programs. In 2013 he presented a series of programs from Afghanistan for the Fairfax Radio network. He has received multiple awards for his work, and is now a host on talk radio 2UE 954 in Sydney, a regular on TV, and writes for The Daily Telegraph.

Klaas Woldring, Ph. D.

Retired A/Prof of Southern Cross University, Lismore (1999), taught Government and Management subjects. Foundation member of Beyond Federation. Migrated from the Netherlands 1959, employed in hospitality industry Netherlands, Southern and Central Africa; re-migrated to Australia in 1964, employed 4.5 years in Chevron Hilton Hotel; then 29 years in tertiary institutions as an academic; married, four children, nine grandchildren. Published: *Beyond Political Independence* (Zambia), Mouton 1984; *Business Ethics in Australian and New Zealand*, ITP Nelson (1996); *AUSTRALIA: Republic or US Colony?* Lulu, (2005); *How about OUR Republic?* BookSurge (2006); *Australia Reconstructed – Bold steps to improve voter representation and the political landscape,* eBook BookPod/ Amazon (2013).

www.beyondfederation.org.au

www.ingramcontent.com/pod-product-compliance
Lightning Source LLC
Chambersburg PA
CBHW072241270326
41930CB00010B/2224